The Mother's Survival Guide

Shirley L. Radl

STEVE DAVIS PUBLISHING
Dallas, Texas

Cover design by Gary DiGiovanni

ISBN 0-911061-19-3
Library of Congress Catalog Card Number 89-50907

STEVE DAVIS PUBLISHING
P.O. Box 190831
Dallas, Texas 75219

Contents

About the Author

Shirley L. Radl is the author of several books about parenting and women's issues, including *Mother's Day Is Over, The Invisible Woman, Over Our Live Bodies,* and, with Dr. Philip G. Zimbardo, *The Shy Child.* She has also written articles on parenting for *American Baby, The Ladies' Home Journal,* and *Family Circle.* Ms. Radl has been a full-time wife and mother of two children, a full-time worker outside the home, and a community activist. She founded the Parental Stress Hotline in Palo Alto, California.

Preface

I feel that many of us go into motherhood with the expectation that we will always feel wonderful about every aspect of the role. This is due in part to the image of motherhood that has been painted by the media: glamorous, fun, and always fulfilling. There are childbirth classes to prepare us for birth, parenting classes to teach us how to take care of the baby, and hundreds of books on nutrition and child development. But few of these prepare us for the days when we don't like being mothers, nor do they tell us how to deal with the guilt we feel when we think we are less than perfect parents.

The names of some of the television shows we watch and some of the products we see advertised may have changed since this book was originally published in 1979. What has not changed, however, is the overall cultural image of motherhood that is the end result of the combined orchestration of the giddy media standards and the prognostications of experts who are often safely away from the action. What also has not changed is the guilt felt by mothers when reality for them falls short of the cultural standards.

Whether it's *The Brady Bunch* or *The Cosby Show*, the TV image of parenthood still involves big, happy families living without care in nice, big houses that are always neat and clean. The song remains the same: motherhood is easy, delightful, rewarding, and there are no dark sides. And, oh yes, there is always an endless supply of money.

The same holds true for the commercials, then and now. Her clothes and hairstyles may have changed, but it is still Mom who scrubs the toilet bowl, becomes euphoric at the effectiveness of a new tile cleaner, and takes immense pride in her whiter-than-white wash. And, because she adores her family, she is fulfilled by housework—but then, it's a real snap if she uses the right products. The commercials, however, do contain a grain of truth: whether a mother works outside the home or not, it is usually she who has the burden of keeping the house. The only real cultural change that has taken place is that society now allows mothers to work two jobs instead of one—largely because most mothers must now work out of financial need.

When I originally wrote this book, my intent was to dispel the silly and dangerous myths about motherhood that contribute to maternal madness. The intent in reissuing it remains the same, since, thanks to the media, those myths are bigger and better than ever. I remain convinced that if mothers can laugh at the myths and stop trying to measure up to the impossible standards that have been set for them, everyone will be happier and healthier for the effort.

Shirley L. Radl

1
There Is Light at the End of the Tunnel

The payoff, other than an occasional total surprise as to my children's endless ingenuity, energy, and aliveness, is elusive. Perhaps once they are grown and there's nothing left of me, I'll be able to feebly pat myself on the back. It reminds me of the traditional gold watch presented at retirement. I'd rather not have it!

Jamie and Chris's
mother

I have three wonderful children, nine, four, and three. I love them so much, and miss them so badly on the days I work. But when I'm with them I scream, smack, and have even kicked my children. I've deliberately broken their toys and run screaming from the house threatening to leave forever. And I was going to be such a wonderful mother!

Tracy, Hughie and
Kevin's mother

They say it's better if you've been married for several years and are past twenty-five before you start your family. While this may be true for people in general, it certainly wasn't for me. It seems that during the eight years after marrying that I eagerly awaited the day when I'd become a mother, the passage of time brought growth to my illusions about what the role would involve. Like Walter Mitty, the longer I was at it, the wilder the fantasies got.

I had visions of having a wonderful pregnancy because I was healthy and had such a sterling attitude toward having children. I would wear chic maternity clothes that I, domestic goddess that I was, would sew with my own hands, and I would, of course, be radiant. The birth would go so perfectly that I'd hop right off the delivery table and walk back to my room, where I'd eat a hearty meal and astonish an entire maternity ward staff with my vigor and good cheer. The baby would be beautiful (occasionally when I got very carried away I fantasized about how wonderful it would be to have *twins*).

We would bring him home to a color-coordinated nursery that mother had decorated herself. Daily, while he was still a baby, I'd lovingly bathe and dress him in precious baby clothes—spotless, of course. *We'd* breastfeed, and I would make all his other baby food with my own hands. Afternoons would be spent sitting in the rocking chair and holding and cuddling him while singing lullabies (the fact that I'm virtually tone deaf never surfaced in my fantasies).

As my child grew, I'd teach him to swim, we'd go on wonderful picnics and other outings together, visit the zoo often, and because of my vast understanding of children, I'd guide him well (*never* shout or spank) and speak to him in Childrenese. Perhaps as he got older, we'd both learn to ride horseback, and we would have great times together trotting over the beautiful rolling foothills of Los Altos and Palo Alto on beautiful sunny afternoons (no doubt to the strains of Glen Yarborough singing "One More Round").

Often during my daydreams I would find myself thinking of

all the things I'd be able to do once maternity freed me from the office and put me into the home. I would finish off the brick terrace we were working on, plant a rose garden, make new curtains or new clothes whenever I felt like it, see all my friends, read all the books that were backlogged, take up drawing and painting, prepare fabulous gourmet meals for my husband, and finally be the perfect woman I was destined to be. For the first time in my married life I truly would be a wife to my husband and see to his and our child's every need.

My husband's shirts would be ironed by loving hands, his socks darned, and he would come home from work every evening to a fulfilled woman, recently freshened up for his arrival instead of one who showed wear and tear after working in an office all day. And, of course, our house would remain as uncluttered as in our child-free years—would sparkle more, in fact.

Whenever I envisioned myself as a housewife and mother, my ideas were so far out that they could have come from a Hollywood script writer or a Madison Avenue advertising conference. Indeed, they probably did.

Although traditional motherhood has taken a few brickbats in recent years, the motherhood myth remains pretty much what it has been for the last thirty years—variations on a theme from *Father Knows Best, The Brady Bunch,* and television commercials for peanut butter. The message is that motherhood is fun, easy, fulfilling, natural, and the capstone of every woman's life. Most women, therefore, come to the state with rather unrealistic expectations of the sort of mothers they will be and the sort of children they will have, without first being given an honest job description of what they're getting into.

Thus, it can come as a shock to a new mother when she finds that she isn't thrilled at being on call on a twenty-four-hour-a-day basis, having her sleep interrupted, or having her nerves ravaged by the noise and confusion that small children can generate. Because she is a thinking person she may have expected a certain amount of work and some of it not at all that pleasant, but no one ever suggested that there would be times when she didn't like being a mother and wished she could send the baby back.

And as a baby grows into a child, a mother soon learns that breakfast—at least in *her* kitchen—isn't exactly like a Tang commercial. Depending on the ages of the children, instead of food being ingested, it may be flung on the wall or on mother— or roll down mother's back in the form of vomit. Three-year-olds don't always drink their milk or juice, but sometimes use it to gargle with or paint pictures on the table. Spirited children frequently bang on the table and scream quite a lot—child-guidance manuals tell us that this is not bad behavior, while friends and relatives tell us it is.

After breakfast, there are faces to be washed, diapers to be changed, and clothes to be put on small people who don't want to wear clothes. Then it is time to keep them out of the bathroom, off the drainboard, and generally out of harm's way. If she is a traditional mother and is at home instead of at work (in which case she will do all this later), while supervising and protecting, mother stokes the washer and dryer, cleans up the kitchen table and floor, washes dishes, makes beds, picks up toys, and cleans toilets.

If she has errands to run, she usually takes any children she has along with her. On the way, she may put a child in the back of the car and experience having the back of her seat kicked all the way to the market. When there are two or more children, she may referee sparring matches while trying to maneuver in traffic. At the supermarket, the journey may be highlighted when her three-year-old flips the rope that holds hundreds of magazines in place or extracts a bottom can from the Del Monte display.

Once home, lunch is a replay of the breakfast scene. Afterward, if mother is fortunate, her children will nap, giving her time to pursue her own interests, such as scraping lunch off the wall, ironing, folding clothes, and mopping the floor . . . again.

Or, exhausted, she may decide to forgo the chores and take this time to catch up on her rest. And she may, as a woman I know did, be awakened from her nap by having her four-year-old (who was supposed to be napping) come in and drop a bean in her ear and wind up in the emergency ward of the hospital to have it removed.

When the children get up from their naps, mother can follow the advice of parental pundits and spend some quality time with them. She might take them to the park, and while there, enjoy the company of other mothers who alternate between reading Bruno Bettelheim and discussing toilet-training and preschool. It is here, while listening to the others, that she may learn that her child is slow in specific areas of development or that his general behavior is abnormal.

After an hour or so, it is time to return home and prepare for father's arrival. There mother prepares dinner while keeping the children off the roof and out of the street, discouraging the unrolling of whole rolls of paper towels, and possibly breaking up arguments that routinely develop between siblings close in age.

When father comes home, depending on how mother's day has gone, he may make his way through an obstacle course of toys, stepping on raisins and Rice Krispies along the way and bearing witness as one of his children discovers that kitchen drawers can be turned into stairways that lead to the drainboard. Chances are father will then take refuge in the living room behind his newspaper, safely away from the action in the kitchen. And depending on what sort of man he is, he may hold the view that traditional motherhood is a lark and inquire of his wife, "What have you been doing all day?"

Working mothers have even more demanding discoveries to make about motherhood. Perhaps it is the notion, held by many husbands, some prospective young mothers, and the culture generally, that motherhood is *indeed* a lark that keeps *working* mothers even more invisible than those who stay at home, and keeps the fact of their working *two* jobs instead of one a bit of a secret. There are answers to the dilemma of working mothers, and I will explore some possible ones subsequently. But I do believe that the underlying reason the plight of the working mother has never been fully aired is that the consensus is that motherhood is easy, that there is virtually no pain or work in the every-day of it, that there are no dark places, that children are wonderful and working mothers are lucky to have them. Perhaps, too, the fact that many working mothers are defensive about their working keeps the lid on. How can they complain about how difficult it is to combine motherhood and a job outside when they should be home taking care of their children in the first place?

Before my children were born, I had an alternate fantasy to my traditional one. While I really did look forward to being a full-time homemaker for the first time in my life, I thought about what it would be like to return to work (in fact, when I was about to have my first child, I kept that door open by taking a maternity leave instead of resigning). And when I pictured myself as a working mother, the image that came to mind was of me sitting at my desk, doing my work during the day, and then later having dinner with my husband and children and afterward reading stories to the kids, or with the entire family playing games together. I did *not* picture myself getting up at five-thirty in the morning (although I knew working mothers who did), getting a baby dressed and fed, taking him or her to the sitter, and at the end of my workday, starting in on another demanding job—made more demanding than in my childless days because of a baby.

Before motherhood, I saw two distinct images: the joy of my future homemaking at a leisurely pace and being out in the world doing my thing. And in neither was there guilt, pain, frustration, disappointment, sick children, or exhaustion. And while my stint at traditional motherhood was a real eye-opener, going back into the working world when my children were preschoolers was a complete shock to my system. Nothing—absolutely nothing—prepared me for the conflicts I experienced. My whole routine changed dramatically, while my husband's did not—it didn't occur to him that it would or should. In addition to the staggering work load, the guilt over leaving the children, and the worry that something would happen to them, or that they would feel neglected, there was still another very painful conflict. It was more than just worrying about unfinished work when I was home and worrying about unfinished children when I was at work.

At the base of it was the darkest feeling of all—that my duality diminished my children, made them less important than they ought to be. And for one whose gut feeling is that nothing is ever so important as one's children, that was a hell I could not talk about. If I hadn't been able to cry into my pillow at night, there would have been no way to release my feelings at all, and for sure I would have been carted off to the funny farm right then and there.

When I went home again—to stay, or so I thought—I went home to the hidden underside of traditional motherhood. I cannot say, even to this day, if my outside job had set me up to flip out, or if going home and trying over again to emulate the cultural ideal and seeing myself as an utter disaster was ultimately responsible. Whatever, I went bonkers.

I have found, through several years of talking and listening to them, that different mothers reach the ends of their ropes at different times. A few have told me that the open-endedness and responsibility of motherhood caused them to feel desperation right from the start, and that it was something that continued to grow—that the pressures just built until they felt as if they were being crushed under the weight of them. The most common reason given for going mad in the early days of motherhood was the incessant crying of the baby. One normally very gentle woman, her nerves battered beyond the limits of her endurance, said that she was just "inches away" from putting a pillow over her baby's face to make him stop crying when she ran from the room and called the pediatrician. Talking to him snapped her out of her madness. Another mother told me that she spanked her six-month-old daughter, which she knew to be absolutely irrational because you don't get a baby to stop crying by inflicting pain.

Other mothers, who didn't experience crying babies or weren't damaged by the storm, had their first sense of being abused when their babies turned into mischievous toddlers or balky two-year-olds. One such woman told me that one evening she said to her husband, "You know, I think it's just possible that we actually have a perfect child," and two weeks later couldn't stand to be in the same room with that particular child.

Child development books have long told mothers that certain behaviors could be expected at certain ages, while child guidance books have offered suggestions for gentle discipline. But none of these has told mothers how to deal with *their* feelings when a young child overturns the kitchen garbage can, throws toys down the toilet, or urinates in a laundry basket full of freshly folded clothes—all on the same day. Nor did anything they had read tell them how to deal with their feelings when constant interruptions and noise caused their powers of concentration to disintegrate. And nothing prepared them for the distinct possibility that they might be so driven they'd feel like slapping a child silly.

Most of the mothers I talked to agreed that all of the nice-sounding theories and suggestions for "communicating" were of no use to them because they couldn't remember them when they were in the middle of a crisis. And most also agreed that it took about five years of continual chaos, confusion, and feelings of inadequacy for them to reach their breaking points. That reconciles rather nicely with sociologist Jessie Bernard's contention that it takes only about five years of motherhood to completely break someone.

When I look back to that time, I was right on schedule. After about five years, my internalized cultural standard for what it took to be a good mother had clashed routinely enough with daily reality so that I was completely beaten down. My sense of humor had vanished. Time stood still. This was the way my life would always be. I was but a vending machine whose function it was to dispense any and all services at the push of a button—and I was one machine that was badly in need of repair.

"Reaching the point where it all has become too much to bear," a young mother of two children told me, "is being constantly with young children and having to bear witness to their every deed, answer questions, take care of sick children, take care of children when you *are* sick, give love whether you feel like it or not, and almost never having a moment's peace or some time alone; it is realizing that you are important only because your children need you, and feeling at the same time as if you are incapable of meeting their needs."

"The breaking point," said another mother, "comes with the accumulation of feeling irritation, frustration, anger, resentment, guilt, and anxiety on a nearly daily basis. It is made worse by never being able to say you feel this way."

"It is flipping out," a mother of three children under the age of five told me. "I went into a deep depression when my youngest child was a year old. This lasted for two years. The only reason for my state that I ever could give to doctors, social workers, and group leaders in therapy sessions was the tension that had built over those years of being a mother of young children. This simply was not accepted."

It is also the feeling that the whole world is watching as you blunder along and that you are going to be held personally accountable for every one of your children's problems or acts of misbehavior.

I remember with clarity the day my life began to look brighter to me. I had gone to lunch with my sister, and afterward we decided to take a drive through the Stanford campus. We were heading in the direction of the beautiful Stanford Chapel. The sun hit the exquisite mosaic on its face in such a way that it shone like millions of jewels. "What a really beautiful sight," I said. And then it occurred to me that it had been a very long time since I'd really noticed the beauty in anything much at all. I felt like rejoicing, but I also felt a strange emptiness when I realized that my depression was leaving—it was, after all, familiar.

A few nights later I walked a neighbor child home after she'd had dinner with us. Her small hand held mine as fondly as mine held hers. It was a beautiful spring evening, and on our way,

Kathy and I smelled the blossoms and picked constellations out of the lovely starry sky.

Six years ago I could never have noticed the sun hitting the chapel and be held in awe at such a sight, and there was no way I could have seen an evening stroll with a seven-year-old child as anything other than still another small, burdensome chore. Nor could I have returned home and enjoyed the freshness of my own two children who had been dispatched to their showers before I took Kathy home—loving the way they smelled and saying, "I love you," without any reservations, and listening as they wound down their day. I love my children. I feel that somehow, a few years back, I was given a second chance with them and have since then been able to enjoy them. But had I not seen that chance and had I continued denying the fact that I didn't absolutely relish the motherhood role, as the motherhood mystique would have you believe every normal mother does every moment, I surely would have missed any pleasure at all in being Lisa and Adam's mother. The day I faced the fact that there really are terrible sides to parenthood was a new beginning for me—the beginning of self-acceptance, growth, and the rebuilding of my rapidly vanishing self-esteem. It was also a beginning for reaching out and grabbing those joyous times and cherishing them before they got away or got buried, and a time for laughter mixed in with the tears.

Four weeks after I started writing about my negative feelings in my first book, *Mother's Day Is Over*, which is an unvarnished job description of the role of wife and mother, marked four weeks of dealing with the conflicts and ambiguities of being a mother. My son was then five years old, and it was at this point that his teacher asked me if any major changes had taken place at home. When I asked why she asked, she said, "I have seen a dramatic change in Adam. A month ago he was a bewildered, inattentive,

nervous child. He is calmer, happier, and more at peace now."
So was I. Or at least I was beginning to be.

It was not just that writing about my feelings had a cathartic
effect that made me feel better (which it did), it was that facing
my problems and knowing that it wasn't unusual for someone
not to love every part of being a mother changed my attitude
toward myself, which changed my attitude toward the children.
My becoming secure made them feel secure. My honest admis-
sion to myself that I didn't always like being a mother, that it
was driving me crazy, led to finding a deeper truth and one that
allowed me to stop hating myself. Underlying my conflicts,
guilts, fear, and resentment was an enormous gap between my
long-held absurd perceptions of what motherhood was supposed
to be like and what it actually was for me. Instead of being
abnormal or evil, I had been mistaken—in the extreme—and
had set myself up for continuing failure.

I was able to see that parenthood isn't all that it's cracked up
to be—and not see such a conclusion as a reflection of my feelings toward my children—but merely what it is: a statement
about the motherhood role. More truths followed, more realistic
attitudes formed, and as I developed stronger emotional resources, health was gradually but steadily restored to this family. This is the story of that journey, one I hope I can help other
similarly conflicted mothers take.

I *have* found a few answers and I learn—from other mothers—
of new ones each day. None of them is relevant for every one of
us. I can't, for example, suggest ways for a mother of a handicapped child to deal with her child or her feelings about her
situation—I have had enough to contend with just dealing with
two children who are thus far perfectly healthy. Nor can I help
a mother whose major problem might be that she is married to
a tyrant who beats her—the temptation would be too strong to

tell her to run away, but I have not walked in her shoes and have no idea why leaving might seem a worse alternative to being knocked around. I couldn't, for that matter, give any advice to a woman whose husband is so unfair and domineering as to never want her to follow her own star.

I am the most average of middle class mothers, and the problems I have had and my ways of dealing with them are restricted to that frame of reference. The only thing that may possibly set me apart from other middle class mothers is that after about five years of parenthood, I came unglued—just because I *was* a mother. And the only thing that might set me apart from mothers who have gone crazy and stayed there is that I turned it around, and did so without years of intensive and expensive therapy. I hit a point and said, "No more!" I figured out why being a mother was sending me down the path to the madhouse and then took steps to reverse the process.

I will always be an anxious mother, but once I fully realized that anxiety is an integral part of caring parenthood, I stopped being anxiety-ridden over my anxiety. The same goes for all the negative emotions I came to know are natural ones for a parent—and particularly the parents of our generation—to feel.

Most of the more than 1,800 books in print on parenting focus on how to care for children, the needs of children, and how to solve specific and universal disciplinary problems. If they acknowledge that a mother has needs *too* and touch on the unhappier emotions she might feel, they do so only lightly. These books are handy, but they are job-training manuals, providing mothers with fewer answers than they can get from their pediatricians or their own mothers—or from some of their more experienced friends. This book is different. It is the one I would like to have had from the beginning to help me maintain my perspective, and hence my sanity. I see it as an important missing link—something that goes between birth and guidance. It covers what most of us should know from the very beginning of motherhood—to throw out the myths and "shoulds" and replace them with fidelity to ourselves and common sense.

While I was looking for ways to put my own house in order, I came upon several programs that are used for restoring families to health after they have been torn apart by crisis. The most unique aspect of these programs is that they are *parent*-centered instead of child-centered. It was immediately obvious that if these programs could help families in crisis, their philosophies and methods could also be used to avert crisis *before it happened*. The more I learned, the more I felt that this knowledge had to be made as public as possible. Thus, throughout this book, I will share with you what I learned from these programs and their application, and what ideas they and their participants inspired in me.

If anyone had told me early in my motherhood that my feelings, no matter how unorthodox, were as valid and important as my children's, and that it wasn't necessary to put a value of right or wrong on *having* them, it would have made sense. I could have avoided an enormous amount of silent suffering. And if it had been borne in upon me that I counted as a person—*not* just in terms of the services I rendered to my family—I would have understood that in order to be a successful and loving parent, I needed to be loved, and that treating myself well is, first, a valid thing to do because I am a human being and, next, that unless I take good care of myself I won't be able to take good care of my children.

And when I recall a day when I was overwhelmed by housework, children, confusion, and a sense of powerlessness over my life, if someone had told me that there was light at the end of the tunnel—that my whole life would not be exactly as it was on that day, and had been for months and months before, it would have made a difference in my attitude. I think it would have helped to get me through that terrible day with just a little hope instead of a sense of dread of the next one.

Motherhood will never be perfect. But *believe me,* it *does* get better! I found that out. I also found out that it is not enough simply to say, "Take heart—remember that light at the end of the tunnel," so along with that glimmer of hope I offer some tried-and-proven suggestions for coping with *your feelings,* whether you are being driven out of your mind by a crying infant or up the wall by a sassy ten-year-old. There are ways to resist some of the pressures that make life painful, to prevent crisis, to have breathing space, and to build and maintain high self-esteem—and enjoy being a mother on a realistic level that permits us to step down from the pedestal past generations have insisted we occupy.

While advice on communicating with your children, disciplining them, and enriching their lives may be well warranted and useful, first you cope. You don't put a roof on a shaky foundation; instead you stabilize that foundation from the ground up and then make improvements to the whole structure. And this is what I hope this book will do—stabilize the foundation by helping other mothers, such as I, who are living through the New Motherhood, to cope with *their* feelings as they look for specific ways to guide and discipline their children. The purpose of this book, then, is to fill what I see as a serious gap in the literature and the tools that are presently offered to us mothers.

2

How to Escape the
What-Will-People-Think Trap

I went from college to marriage, and the thing to do was have a baby. You weren't really married unless you had a baby. We love our daughter very much, but how different our lives would be if we were childless. But at the time, we couldn't withstand the pressure of family and friends.

Now that our daughter is in school, things are better. Except that people keep saying, "Well, it's about time you had a playmate for your little girl."

Terry's mom

The thing is, I fell for the whole thing—hook, line, and sinker. I feel so dumb. So taken.

My family hasn't turned out to match my fantasies and that has almost destroyed us with guilt and made me think that everyone else was reaping rewards I was never to have.

I love my children, but I don't like this role. I'm afraid to say that to anyone because they'd think I was a loony.

Bitter

Is there a shadow of a doubt that social pressure that is strong enough to turn a woman into a mother—effect the most important decision she will ever make—will, often without her realizing it, continue to influence her long after the physical fact of motherhood is a reality? The pressures that are applied to a young woman to have children, however, are nothing compared to those that will come from all sides once she has succumbed to the combined orchestration of the mass media and her friends, relatives, and acquaintances. All of the myths and pressures that were internalized prior to motherhood remain, and after they have helped to push her into motherhood, they turn into a club that can beat her senseless.

How Heeding the Opinion of Others Can Drive Us Up the Wall

The following is just one of many letters I've received that vividly illustrate the full impact of social pressure on women:

I was married for five years before we started our family. By the time we did, I'd just about had it with people telling me I shouldn't wait too long to have a baby, or asking if something was wrong with me, of if my work was taking the place of my natural instincts as a woman. I felt I had to prove something— not just that I could have a baby, but that once I did, I'd be a better mother than everyone who had been bugging me for all those years.

But I'd had to defend myself—or at least I felt I had to—for not having children for so long that I carried that feeling over. I felt that everyone was watching me, just waiting for me to goof. When my first baby cried, it bothered me. But when other people were around, it bothered me more. I remember when he was two years old and he misbehaved and made noise in front of other people, I felt ashamed of him.

I counted so much on him to help me show everyone that I wasn't inadequate that I expected too much of him. He was not a superbaby, which made me not a supermother, and I resented him. I couldn't admit that to anyone because that would only confirm their suspicions that I was a bad mother.

I'll never forgive myself for the way I treated him—yelling at him and slapping him—during the first three years of his life. All because I didn't want people to think my child was a brat.

Another woman, *quite literally* concerned with appearances, had this to say to Dear Abby:

I gave birth to a healthy baby girl ten months ago. My husband and I very much wanted this baby, but I have proven . . . to be a very immature and rotten mother.

You see, the baby is very homely. She has a large nose—every time I look at her I start crying.

I don't want to take the baby out where people can see her because someone is sure to see what a big nose she has and I will be embarrassed.

This is ruining my whole life. I went to a psychiatrist for several months, but I quit going because he refused to believe it was really the baby's nose that bothered me . . .

I have a wonderful husband and wonderful parents and I feel that I have let them all down because I'm such a terrible mother. I wanted this baby so much, but she isn't giving me any happiness at all. I felt so guilty for being ashamed of her looks.

Isolation, which is already built into the contemporary nuclear family motherhood role, even if a woman works, can be deadly. Because this mother is ashamed of her baby and her feelings, in her motherhood hours she's cutting herself off even more—which should give you some idea of how valuable the good opinion of other people is to her. She has fully internalized the idea that it is not socially acceptable to have an ugly baby. And that it is even less socially acceptable to *say* you have one or feel unhappy about it.

Why We Really Punish in Public

Richard Peairs, co-author (with Lillian Peairs) of *What Every Child Needs,* believes that children are punished in public so that onlookers will think well of the parents. In an interview, he recalled witnessing a small incident at a bank. "A little boy, maybe four years old, was fascinated by the velvet rope (which marked the customer's line) and started swinging on it. His mother screwed up her face and screamed at him, 'Bad.' I think she was trying to show us what a good parent she was—not letting him get away with anything . . . "

His point may be well taken, but Peairs's assessment would have been more on the mark had he speculated on how this mother might have been regarded by others had she gently reasoned with the child, as Spock advises, and been unsuccessful in her attempts to get him to leave the rope alone. Chances are that Peairs and the other witnesses to the scene would have concluded that this was a permissive, indulgent parent and her child a spoiled brat. And from what *I've* seen at the supermarket, this example was quite mild. I've seen children nearly flogged because their parents were getting sidelong glances from other shoppers with "Can't-you-control-your-child?" expressions etched on their disapproving faces.

Mess

Something else that triggers punishment that really doesn't fit the crime is mess. There are three reasons why people are fussy about the condition of their homes: they can't stand mess, or they resent having to clean up after others and nag those others into cleaning up after themselves, or they want everything to look right in the event that someone should drop by. It is the last reason that concerns me, for mothers have been known to rail at their children, not so much because the mess bothers them but because they want always to make a good impression on other people—sometimes people they don't even like or respect and whom they wish wouldn't drop by at all.

Foul Language

When children first go to school they start to pick up foul language and experiment with it. We are told by nearly everyone on the face of the earth that we parents shouldn't make a big deal over this because if the children get the idea that it bothers us, they'll just do it more to get a reaction out of us. But parent after parent still responds—sometimes violently. Why? One mother provides us with an answer not unfamiliar to many of us. When her five-year-old came home from kindergarten and uttered "*that* horrible word," she washed his mouth out with soap, took his pants down and spanked him on his bare bottom, and sent him to his room. She was mortified that her son had used such language, "right out there in the street for all the neighbors to hear—my God, what must they think of us?" For the record, it should be noted that this mother has been known to use *that* word, which illustrates rather nicely that parents get uptight over things that don't actually make *them* uptight, but which they assume make other people uptight.

First in the Class

Sometimes, parents who give in to peer pressure that says you will be regarded in direct relation to the performance of your children hide their motivation even from themselves, seeing the pressure they put on their children as loving interest. Nowhere is this more evident than in the classroom. For example, a second-grade teacher, the father of several children himself, told me, "Kids are under great pressure to achieve. Not just to learn and do well in school, but always to get straight A's. This is so important to many parents that they are blind to what this does to their kids. The parents in our school seem to be competing with each other—they all want intellectual geniuses they can be proud of and what they are winding up with instead is a bunch of nervous children."

When my daughter was having trouble with her math I mentioned this to the mother of one of her classmates. She immediately gave me the names of three tutors and two psychiatrists, explaining that her son had also had "serious problems," so she hired a tutor at $15 an hour and took him to a couple of psychiatrists for reasons she never explained. The "serious problems" he was having, she later revealed, boiled down to the fact that the boy was getting C's in math. Of course, her concern is understandable, and of course, she was right in hiring a tutor to help her son. And now that I think about it, pulling a C in Palo Alto could constitute a "serious problem," requiring two psychiatrists to no doubt confirm this mother's fear that underlying her son's problem was one or another of her deficiencies.

I've been told of a twelve-year-old girl whose parents beat her when her grades drop. She is said to be a frightened child, given to fits of depression. I'm aware that, until recently, the parents of some of my daughter's classmates made it a practice to type their children's reports neatly, "editing" them along the way, so that they would wind up on display at Open House.

I first noticed this when Lisa was in the fourth grade. A parent standing next to me, admiring the work on the table, said, "I didn't know they taught kids this young to type. Isn't that wonderful? I wonder why they didn't teach my James to type." We looked at each other for a moment and then both said, "Ah, so!" And after reading a couple of reports that were written at about the high school level, we agreed that we should register a protest. As an aside, I would like to add here that I thought *my* protest was rather stunning. At the time I was involved in a project that had me using an IBM composer to set type. My daughter had just finished doing a report and I told her I wanted to type it for her. I edited it and then set it up in type, with justified margins on both sides no less. Shortly thereafter a memorandum was issued to class parents, informing us that typed papers were no longer acceptable.

It is often difficult to be sympathetic toward parents who apply undue pressure on their children to achieve, are dishonest, or actually cruel, just so they will be well thought of because of their children's accomplishments. But, on the other hand, as psychologist Ann Koch points out, parents often suffer the brunt of their children's behavior and are criticized by teachers, family, and friends. Mrs. Koch, who is the director of a program for hyperactive children in Palo Alto, said in an interview that parents of hyperactive children "are told they should be tougher and get their act together." She believes instead that hyperactive children are hard to handle and that parents' instincts are often correct but become distorted through society pressure. In my opinion, Mrs. Koch's conclusions may well be applicable whether or not a child is hyperactive—parents of *all* children are held accountable and are thus extremely self-conscious regarding their children's performance.[1]

The *One* Job on Which Everyone Is an Expert But You

And why not? Most mothers are aware that everyone from the President of the United States to the checker at the supermarket has an opinion on how they should do their jobs. And in between there are the child guidance experts who tend to give out the message that there is a solution for every problem—the underlying cause for which *is mother*.

In the beginning, if a child cries a lot it's because his mother doesn't hold him enough because she's away at work, or is at home and holds him too much and is spoiling him, or doesn't change his diaper often enough. When he reaches six months of age, if he isn't sitting up then obviously there's something wrong with him. If he doesn't crawl "on time" or isn't taking his first steps as he marks his first birthday, the same judgment holds. And if a child isn't fully toilet-trained at two, there's something wrong with him, his mother, or both. And what if, God forbid, the child does disgusting things such as spreading his feces on the wall? (I wonder how many people know that this is perfectly normal behavior for a child under the age of two?)

What will people think, a mother may ask herself, if they know that my baby's crying drives me up the wall—that I don't care as much about *why* he's crying as I do about what it's doing to *my* nervous system? What will they think when I use a harness on my two-year-old because I can't control him in public? Will they understand that I'm concerned about his safety, or will they think I'm treating him like an animal? What will the pediatrician think of me when he sees my baby's diaper rash? What will he think if the baby misbehaves? Will he think I'm either spoiling or neglecting him? Certainly if my child isn't clean and dry and wearing lovely baby clothes, he'll think I'm an uncaring mother. What will people think when they see my child with a pacifier? What will they think when he sucks his thumb? What will my friends think if I return to work? What will *some* of them think if I don't?

And on and on, no doubt not even letting up once one's offspring are in their middle years. It is absurd to the point of being laughable. But it isn't funny because it's true and it can drive mothers crazy. Worse yet, as I pointed out earlier, it can lead a parent to harshly and unfairly discipline or punish a child—not because the child went against a parent's standard, but because he or she behaved in a way that a mother *may think* makes *her* look bad in the eyes of others. When this sort of concern is extreme, it can actually be dangerous. For example, one social worker who has spent many years working to prevent child abuse told me that parents who have the most serious problems are the ones who are inclined to worry the most over appearances. Sharrol Munce Blakely developed and coordinated the Children's Trauma Center at Children's Hospital in Oakland, California. She also served as director of the Office of Child Abuse during the administration of former California Governor Jerry Brown. In numerous conversations, we discussed this aspect of parental stress. Most pointedly, on one such occasion, she told me, "Ironically, people often get into stress situations because they are overly concerned about how other people view them as parents and they might wind up hurting a child who lets them down, only to worry about what other people will think of *that.*"

And I rather suspect that there are many people who, having reached this point, need professional counseling but don't seek it because they don't want people to think they're crazy or incapable of dealing with their own problems.

Escaping the What-Will-People-Think Trap

So what's a mother to do if she is locked into partially believing the motherhood myth and caught in the what-will-people-think trap?

First and foremost, having been there myself, I strongly urge all parents to lower their sights to a realistic level. Remember that children are not born civilized—civilizing them is one *long* and *very repetitious* process.

Having been a parent who had so little self-confidence that I felt that someone was always looking over my shoulder and recording every trivial error I made, as well as any of my children's flaws, I must say to others, don't make the same mistake. Don't care *too much* about how you might appear to other people—or *think* you might appear.

It is okay if you and your child or children are imperfect. It is okay to admit that you fall short of the cultural ideal, make mistakes, and sometimes don't even like being a parent. But what will other people think if you admit to such weaknesses? First, you have more company than you think. Next, you are likely to learn that at least some of the times when you have worried about what other people might be thinking of you, if those other people also happened to be mothers, they may have been too busy worrying about what sort of impression *they* were making on *you* to notice any of *your* shortcomings. We do not actually *know* what everyone else is thinking—we only think we do, and quite often we are completely mistaken.

There are, of course, people in the world who will judge you given any opportunity. Their pleasure in life seems to lie either in coercing others into conformity and agreement or being instrumental in arousing feelings of guilt in other people. And what is so insidious about them is their power. First, we tend to notice any reinforcement that we are inadequate *more* than we do affirmation of our abilities; nine of your friends, for example, could quietly approve of the way you run your life (or not concern themselves about it), but what will stand out in your mind is the one "friend" who lets it be known that he or she thinks you should be doing things differently—*his* or *her* way.

Next, pressure bearers seem to be stronger in number because they are vocal, while other people who quietly mind their own business seem to recede into the background. This can lead us to mistakenly assume that *everyone* is manipulative and if we cut out those in our lives who are, we will be left without friends.

In his book, *How I Found Freedom in an Unfree World*, Harry Brown says that he thinks that people often maintain relationships with people who make them miserable because they're afraid of being lonely. And then he asks, "Aren't they *very* lonely when they deal with people who don't understand and appreciate them?" Noting that he would be, he continues, "I've also been lonely sometimes while looking for compatible people. But that loneliness was usually short-lived and more than rewarded by the discovery of people who wanted me for what I am. Around them, I am understood and appreciated in a way I never could have been among people with different standards."

"When you find them," Brown reminds us, "you'll have relationships that impose no restrictions upon you. You'll be among people who will want you to be as you are."[2]

An example of how unrelenting the coercive personality can be still remains fresh in my memory. When, a few years back, I finally admitted that what probably turned me into a mother was social pressure and that it also contributed to my general misery during the early years of my motherhood, the one person who had applied more pressure than anyone else said, "How ridiculous—you *shouldn't* have allowed yourself to be so influenced by cultural attitudes and other people. Don't you have a mind of your own?" To the roster of other deficiencies that she had pointed out to me, starting with my previous unwomanliness or selfishness in waiting so long to have children, she could now add that I was weak-minded.

But I did learn something from my relationship with this

person. Of course, she was right. I should never have allowed any of her words to even ever so slightly influence any of my decisions, feelings (usually of inadequacy), or actions. But I can't go back and can only apply what I learned from her (and others) as I move along, and pass it on: namely, people who manipulate you or apply pressure to get you to conform to their standards do not have your best interests at heart. When they pass judgment on you, they in fact bear you ill-will. To bully or insult another person, however genteely, is an act of hostility. People who do this should be avoided whenever possible.

Now, obviously, you can't avoid everyone who would manipulate you. There's your mother-in-law, your Aunt Rose who means well, a neighbor who is otherwise quite helpful, a co-worker. But when they pry into your business, you are under no obligation to offer them any explanation for the way you conduct your life, and you don't have to listen to their unsolicited "advice." You can simply and politely say, "I don't want to talk about it."

It takes practice, of course, to stand up to outside pressure, but each time you do it, it becomes easier and you become stronger. And if you look closely at your need to gain the approval of others in specific areas of life, your attitude can change. You can decide which is more important to *you*—having someone think you are a wonderful disciplinarian or guiding your child in a way that truly reflects *your personal values*. I would prefer, for example, for my children to feel free to express their feelings and be themselves—even if occasionally they shout in front of other people—than to have quiet, polite children who are shy, or who eventually translate "quiet is good" into not being able to talk openly to their parents. Often, I think that "perfectly" behaved children are the ones whose parents say of them when they hit adolescence, "He never talks to me—we just don't communicate." During those early years we lay the groundwork for the relationships we eventually will have with our children. And much of this groundwork is dependent on the expectations we have of our children and the assumptions on which those expectations are based.

But more to the immediate point, I have found that as one gradually learns to stand up to pressure, instead of becoming defensive or submitting, those who apply the pressure start backing off—presumably to look around for easier marks with whom to play their sinister games.

Finally, it is good to remember that no matter what you do you will never receive approval from *everyone*—simply because all people are not in absolute agreement as to what is socially acceptable. Thus, you are bound to receive condemnation or criticism from someone. And when you are out in public and your child misbehaves, as children do, and it embarrasses you, think about why you should care whether perfect strangers may disapprove of you. If, in fact, they even bother to stop thinking about their own concerns long enough to do so!

3

Every Mother's
Early Warning Guide
to Danger Zones

All observers tend to agree that just about the most difficult time in a mother's life is during the first five or six years of her children's lives. This reconciles with the findings of experts such as Dr. C. Henry Kempe, of the University of Colorado Medical Center, who have found that the child most vulnerable to parental violence is the one who is five years old or younger. The reason for this, obviously, is that being with young children 24 hours a day is extremely stressful. They need more care, create more confusion and mess, make more demands, and are not usually in school most of the time but instead are likely to be at home all day—and if they are home with a parent, that parent is usually mother. When that is the case, because of the continual exposure to one another, both the mother and the child are in the most serious danger zone of all.

There are other situations and certain times that often turn out to set the stage for maternal stress. Some are serious, some are trivial, some are obvious, some are not at all apparent. In some cases it is possible for a mother to do something to make a "danger zone" less dangerous for herself and her child. At other times the best she can do is to be aware and post storm warnings to herself. In any case, it is good to be forewarned of some of the problems that follow.

Postpartum Depression

To begin with, it is real. This, from the book *Our Bodies, Ourselves:*

The first stage is the immediate postpartum feeling which we have during our hospital stay. We may feel incredibly high about the actual birth of our baby, and tremendously relieved that there is nothing wrong with him/her . . . and then we come down with a crash, aching from stitches and general weariness. Some of us may not mind the achiness, it being a constant reminder of the hard work we have just completed and feel so good about.

I would like to pause here before going on to the next phase of postpartum depression described in *Our Bodies, Ourselves* and focus on what happens when a woman *doesn't* feel good about the "hard work" of giving birth. While it is gratifying that a current publication does acknowledge that having a baby can be difficult, it comes as a bit of a surprise. The more widely held view these days is that giving birth is always a snap and an experience to end all experiences—with or without the prospect of parenthood and all it entails. I am aware of no less than a half dozen current books on the subject, and in the last couple of years I've read dozens of articles proclaiming the ease and thrill of natural childbirth (more thrilling when it takes place at home is the current message).

I think it is great that women are taking charge of their bodies and the births of their children. It is certainly much healthier than holding still for the sometimes barbaric intervention on the part of those obstetricians who don't see birth as the natural function that it is but, instead, the "crisis" point of a "disease" known as pregnancy. And I applaud men who help their wives (such as those who participate in the Lamaze method and actually aid at the birth).

I like the idea of "prepared birth," but what I don't like is that it doesn't go far enough. That is, most courses do not prepare a woman for its all not coming up roses, or teach them how to deal with it when it doesn't. The current dogma is that childbirth is easy and painless and any woman can jog around the delivery table afterward—*if* she prepares the way she's supposed to and has the proper attitude. The message I get is that if it all doesn't go splendidly there's something wrong with mother—either she didn't do her exercises, wasn't sincere, or has some deep-seated psychological problem that has gotten in the way.

Well . . . I have news. Even house pets—cats and dogs—differ individually when they give birth (Boston terriers frequently have C-sections). Anyway, the new myth of natural, blissful, painless childbirth for everyone is just that—a myth. There will always be complications in some births, always be C-sections, and always be perfectly normal natural childbirth that hurts like hell. And there will always be women who either can't or don't want to breastfeed their babies. And . . . there will always be those who, for whatever reason, choose to lay trips on them and suggest that the measure of a woman is her "success" at natural childbirth and breastfeeding.

I know that a sense of failure can make the postpartum period especially intense. Try not to let that happen. Don't let anyone lay a trip on you if the birth of your baby wasn't perfectly natural or naturally perfect, or breastfeeding didn't work out. And don't lay a trip on yourself. Being able to carry these things off is the result of *luck* and not virtue. I have known perfectly terrible mothers who scored high on these functions and perfectly wonderful ones who didn't. For the record, I had one "success" and one "failure"—one completely normal birth that was so painful that I begged for an anesthetic and one so easy that I feared I'd have the baby in the car on the way to the hospital.

This is a danger zone that shouldn't be one—the birth is ancient history once the baby is here. Moving on past that, again, from *Our Bodies, Ourselves:*

The second stage of postpartum, which may last from one to three months, is the actual coping with ourselves and our new baby once we get home. There is the incredible fatigue that comes from not having an uninterrupted night of sleep; the stress of incorporating this new person into our existing family; our changing role with our mate; along with our baby's constant needs. In addition to exhaustion, we may feel fragmentation, disorientation and chaos. Life seems a blur; we feel little control at the time.[1]

When a woman is suffering from postpartum depression, it's important for her to recognize what it is she's experiencing and not see it as abnormal in any way. Sometimes our pride gets in the way of asking for help from our doctors or other people when this occurs. It's as if to say *"I* never had that experience" is somehow evidence of sterling character when it is simply good fortune. Having help with the baby, if it can be arranged, can make a world of difference.

Separation of Mother and Child

When, because of complications, a mother and a newborn child are separated for any length of time, a coolness, for which no one should feel guilty, can develop between them. The mother does not always quickly develop a way of responding affectionately to the child; the child who is not touched frequently (perhaps it is in an incubator) isn't always quickly responsive on coming home. Birth complications sometimes can cause a mother to have negative feelings toward the child who has caused her so much pain. (Then, of course, she may have added to her burden a sense of failure at having any complications whatsoever.)

Early separation is also a factor with adopted children who are taken from their natural mothers and then not placed with adoptive parents for some weeks—unless they have been cared for by someone who has been able to lavish on them that necessary early affection.

Most pediatricians are aware of this, but some are not; if you have problems in these areas ask your own doctor about them and check with local organizations and hospitals to seek out programs specifically designed to help you bridge the affection gap. And for heaven's sake, don't castigate yourself for having "unmotherly" feelings over which you have no control.

When Your Baby Cries and Cries

Any mother who is constantly subject to noise is in a danger zone—the eye of the storm. Even Margaret Mead was. In *Blackberry Winter*, she wrote:

> *Once when she raged, I found myself stamping my foot in the kind of blind responsive rage a mother can feel when her child screams unappeased. I caught it, realized what it was. Experienced only once, it was enough to make me recognize what lies back of the desperation of a young mother, innocent of all knowledge of babies, who feels she will never be able to cope . . .*[2]

And as Jessie Bernard points out, industrial engineers long have been aware of the fatigue and health hazards of noise pollution. She submits that if the stresses to which a mother is exposed could be measured in a laboratory, monitored, and recorded, "they would be shown as enormous. A crying infant, as any sleep-starved young mother can testify, can be devastating . . .[3]

Further, when there is an older child to deal with, a mother's already strained patience may render her incapable of tolerating any of the older child's antics, and at the slightest irritating act, she may find herself in a blinding rage. Or she may lash out at the small noisemaker or herself.

I have heard experts say that the reason a mother might feel anger at a crying infant is that the crying is an indication that the baby doesn't love her. That is probably true in some cases, but I'm more inclined to feel that a mother who feels anger at a noisy infant or preschooler (or one who may be an innocent bystander) is suffering more from an excess of noise pollution than a sense that her child doesn't love her.

Whatever the dynamics of the situation, there is no reason why a mother should be forced to listen to the noise if she can possibly avoid it. Assuming that she first checks with the doctor to determine that there's nothing wrong or nothing that can be done, she should then take steps to preserve her mental health.

It is far less heartless, for example, for a tortured mother to close the door to a baby's room, use ear plugs, or turn up the stereo full blast than it would be to become so driven and angry that she loses control and winds up striking or shaking a child. If the weather is nice, she can go outside. If you are faced with this situation, don't worry about stepping away from the baby briefly—given the state of mind of any mother whose nerves are being ravaged, the baby is better off safely tucked away in his bed with some distance between baby and mother.

And if to get some peace you leave a noisy baby with someone else for a while, don't feel it is wrong to put this burden on another person; someone else can take it if he or she hasn't been exposed to it for hours on end.

Toilet Training

Although my purpose is not to offer specific child-guidance suggestions, a discussion of toilet training seems appropriate here because it is a cause of serious maternal stress that often leads to severe punishment. And unlike other problems that involve an individual child's behavior that is not to his mother's liking, this is one area of stress that can be avoided entirely.

When my daughter was approaching her second birthday (and my son his first) I started feeling guilty that I hadn't seriously tried to train her. And I was surrounded by people who either chided, "Is that baby *still* in diapers?" or mothers who beamed, "My Stevie was trained at nine months." So feeling an appropriate amount of pressure both from within and without, I set out to train her.

I dragged Spock off the shelf and dragged the potty chair into the bathroom. I routinely watched for some sign that Lisa was ready—as Spock advised—and soon we were spending hours every day in the bathroom. I'd say all the right words and patiently wait, often for thirty minutes or more. Nothing. And then five minutes later, after either her diaper or training pants were in place, nature would quietly take its course. And then about an hour later, or sooner, we'd start in again. And often while I was preoccupied with Lisa, Adam, who was now scurrying around, would seize upon this golden opportunity to explore the great mysteries of the house and get into all sorts of mischief.

At the end of two weeks my patience had evaporated and I was yelling at both children. The house was a mess, I was feeling like a total failure as a mother, Lisa was showing signs of feeling that she was the object of my hatred, while her brother was showing signs of being left out.

And then two things happened. A neighbor told me that when

her daughter was somewhere between two and three years old, she came to her, diaper in hand and said, "I no wanna wear dis," and from that day forth used the potty, with mother's only role being instruction in the use of toilet paper and helping her little girl into her training pants. The next thing that happened was that I saw Dr. Lendon Smith on a television show and he said that toilet training was pointless—that if the parents used the bathroom, the children would follow their example.

That settled it. I put my daughter back in diapers and, instead of sitting her on the seat and waiting for lightning to strike, I simply took her into the bathroom whenever I went. She observed and asked questions, and in no time she made the connection between the sensations in her body and what would follow. Almost immediately, she learned that she could control both her bowels and bladder, and without much ado she took a shine to the potty chair and started using it regularly—and soon she insisted on wearing panties. A year later, Adam was similarly "trained," using as his model his father. His "training" was so uneventful that I have little memory of what actually took place.

I am firmly convinced that toilet training is an exercise in wasted motion. It is an enormous waste of time and emotional energy, it is completely unnecessary—and certainly mothers of young children have enough to do. But far worse is that it is a source of aggravation that can lead to spanking a child for something he or she is not physically mature enough to master.

On or off the pot, children can be exasperating. It should not take too much imagination to understand how volatile a situation can become when a mother feels that she is trapped in the bathroom (while other responsibilities await her) with a balky two-year-old who is becoming balkier from being forced to sit on a pot for what must seem like hours.

The least serious consequence of toilet training is that both you and your child will feel like failures when it doesn't work the way it's supposed to. The most serious is that, as any honest mother will testify, it can lead to violence.

The age at which toilet training normally takes place is *already* a danger zone. The advice from here when you start out on this dubious enterprise is *don't!*

Too Much Patience

A friend of mine, the mother of two children and a psychiatric nurse, says that she believes that one of the reasons some parents blow sky high is that they keep trying to be patient and understanding and don't even realize that the pressures and anger mount with each trivial attack on the senses—until the final straw is in place, and *WHAM!*

Another friend, who exemplifies the patient, serene mother, typically responds to such antics as having her four-year-old ransack the closets, flush her eyeglasses down the toilet, or fling her orange juice across the room with "Don't, sweetheart," adding, "She didn't mean to," or "Here, darling, have some more juice." One day the child accidentally spilled her milk during lunch. It hadn't even started rolling toward the table's edge when her mother slapped her a half dozen times and stopped short of slamming the child into the wall.

Better, I think, to let it out a little bit at a time. A good place to begin might be to dispense with the saccharine and move on to verbally expressing disapproval when it is appropriate. A general rule of thumb is not to punish or castigate children for accidents or clumsiness, but when their behavior goes against your family values, or is inconsiderate of others, deliberately naughty, or malicious, to send them to their rooms. My serene friend, for example, would have been better off scolding her child and sending her to her room when she tossed the towels around, flushed the eyeglasses down the toilet, and flung the juice across the room. Both mother and child would have been better off had she yelled like a *fishwife!* Yelling is a wonderful way to release tensions and convey disapproval, and I hardly think it is damaging to children (unless you regularly hurl demeaning insults), given the fact that they make so much noise themselves.

The Dinner Hour

According to the National Safety Council, most accidents in the home occur around the dinner hour when mothers are exhausted and trying to prepare dinner with hungry children underfoot. According to specialists whose business it is to know, most child-abuse incidents occur at this time. And according to most mothers I've talked to, that's when the fuse reaches its very shortest point of the day.

There are no absolute solutions to the problems the dinner hour may pose, of course, but some suggestions that have been made are that this is a good time for a mother or father to take the children for a walk or drive to the store to pick up some ice cream for dessert while the other parent prepares the meal.

This would work well for homemakers: start early—when the children are outside playing or perhaps when they are napping—and prepare as much of the dinner in advance as possible. Salad greens can be prepared and the table set in the late afternoon before the children are back in the kitchen begging for dinner. Also, whether you prepare early or not, this is a good time to take the phone off the hook. Why, I've always wondered, do people telephone mothers during the dinner hour—when the impatience of hungry children, and perhaps father's imminent arrival, converge with (at least minimal) dinner preparations?

When both parents work, they really should sit down and work out an equitable arrangement that suits their individual needs and tastes. If one of them adores cooking and wants to take on that chore exclusively, this is great, *provided* the other parent takes over with the children and makes sure they aren't underfoot in the kitchen. If both parents *hate* cooking, then neither should get stuck with that chore routinely, but instead it should be shared; similarly, when both like to cook, they can take turns with one cooking and the other keeping children out of range on different nights of the week. Whatever the situation, a parent cooking dinner with children underfoot is in a danger zone. If you can't do anything to change the system in your own home, at least be aware of this.

Breaking Bad Habits

Even something so positive and confidence-building as breaking a smoking habit or going on a diet can put a mother in a danger zone. Dieting makes people cranky and given to bursts of rage (and I wonder how many new mothers, eager to shed pounds gained during pregnancy, realize this). One doctor I spoke with told me that giving up tobacco is more difficult than giving up heroin. Joseph Alsop once refuted the notion that people who have quit smoking don't like to be around people who still smoke—Alsop insists, instead, that people who have stopped smoking just don't like to be around people, period.

So choose the time to break your bad habits or try out a new diet wisely. Several people who have been successful in breaking bad habits or losing weight say that they planned in advance not to do anything else important while trying to achieve their goals, and they emphasized that they chose periods of time when they were most likely to be stress-free.

Marital Stress

When your marriage is under stress, you are in one of the most hazardous of the danger zones. It is not at all unusual for the most loving mother to neglect her children during such a period or to take out her troubles on them. When you are working out marital problems, the children frequently are troubled too, and hence are more edgy.

When You Have a Lot on Your Mind

Heavy preoccupation with anything, but especially with problems, sets up many mothers for domestic fireworks. Not unlike the overly patient mother, a preoccupied person may be temporarily shutting out the confusion of the environment, but it really all is coming through at some level, and when the force of it hits, the impact seems far greater than if the impulses come through at their normal pace. And when a person is in a state of grief, he or she is far more prone to preoccupation and far more vulnerable.

And yet, a mother who is able to distract herself from her pain is not always better off—she is *still* preoccupied. One woman told me that when she was extremely depressed over the death of her mother she finally had been able to get her mind off her grief by thinking about other things: "I was lost in my thoughts about, of all things, redecorating the kitchen, and feeling almost normal again. Then my five-year-old burst into the room, climbed up on the drainboard, and knocked over the cookie jar. When I got angry at him I truly believed it was because of what he had done. Later I realized I hated him—at that moment—for bringing me back to reality."

The Sun and the Moon

There's hardly a mother alive who hasn't known what it is to have the weather play a strong role in her reaching the end of her rope. Rainy, cold, or snowy days that confine active youngsters to the house and virtually glue them to mother's elbow or a blaring TV set are familiar to most of us. These are the days when "I-don't-have-anything-to-do" becomes a tiresome refrain (and days when we might feel a bit guilty for allowing the kids to watch more TV than we think they should). And, of course, when they do unstick themselves and go outside for a while they usually bring in a trail of mud for mom to clean up. On those days we don't recognize the danger soon enough. It just creeps up. Better then to acknowledge at the beginning that it's going to be one of *those* and guard against the possibility before we lose control.

In still another way, the weather plays a greater role than one might think. One mother who was given to moods with her child, exclaimed, "The weather doesn't have to be rainy or dreary. It could be a perfectly beautiful day, and there would be something about it—the clouds, the smell in the air, the color of the sky—that without my being consciously aware of it was very much like a day in my past that was filled with pain. So, without knowing precisely why, I would once again be feeling that same pain. Anyway, while I was in that state if my daughter did anything out of line—no matter how trivial—I would resent it." As this woman spoke, I felt an instant spark of recognition. Since then, when I've had an up or down day for no apparent reason, I've thought about the possibility that the weather was causing me to have a sense of *déjà vu*, and often I can tie in certain emotions with certain kinds of days.

While the idea that the phase of the moon can have certain effects on one's emotions is still generally thought to be mere superstition, it is interesting to note that the San Francisco Police Department routinely doubles its patrol during a full moon—in fact, they start this just a couple of days before the moon is at its fullest and continue the practice for two days afterward. And most radio and TV talk show personalities I've asked about this nervously admit that they get more crank calls during this period than at any other time during the month. Furthermore, the volunteers and counselors who staff crisis intervention hotlines acknowledge that their calls more than double when the moon is full. One social worker at Children's Hospital in Oakland, California, wondering if his department was the only one in the area that could regularly chart the phase of the moon by the number of child-abuse cases they had, did some checking: "I called Stanford Hospital, Kaiser, a couple of hotlines, and a few clinics. All of them said the story was the same." Naturally, this could all be mere coincidence. But whether it is or isn't, it seems a good idea to know that some people really do believe that both parents and children are more given to bizarre behavior at this time.

Furthermore, as reported in *Human Behavior* (February, 1978), Dr. Paul K. Jones and Dr. Susan L. Jones of Case Western Reserve University tabulated the suicides in Cuyahoga County, Ohio, from 1972 through 1975 and then plotted them according to the phase of the moon. They found the suicide rate to be 43 percent higher during a new moon than during other phases.[4]

The Holidays

Beginning with Halloween—actually about a week before for most mothers—we move into the longest danger zone of all—the holidays. Depending on the ages of the children, there are the costumes to deal with, whether or not to have a party, whether or not they need to be chaperoned when they join their friends in trick-or-treating (and if so, which parent will do the chaperoning and which will stay home and hand out the goodies). Once all that is resolved, a mother may feel compelled to make her children's Halloween costumes; decorate the house with cardboard skeletons, witches, and the like; carve batches of pumpkins, save the seeds for roasting (to be served with hot chocolate after the little hobgoblins have brought home sacks of candy); or actually have a bunch of kids in to bob for apples. When anyone eats supper is a mystery—anyone, of course, being the parents, for you feed the children at five because they want to get moving early. Once it's all over then you have to deal with sorting the candy, checking for needle marks, razor blades, or anything you paranoiacally feel some demon may sadistically have inserted for the sheer joy of making a tot suffer. Once you've got it all categorized into safe and unsafe, then you may stew about whether to toss most of it out so that your kids don't get sick on it and ruin their teeth eating it. And Halloween is supposed to be marvelous fun!

My husband and I have learned to psyche ourselves up for this—it is a dreadful time of year. The drive to the pumpkin patch—bumper to bumper, kids fighting in the back of the car—is horrible. The whole hassle over costumes is aggravating, and everything else that follows is absolutely miserable. I've learned not to make costumes and aggravate myself further. We simply try to get through the night. Many parents, incidentally, have told me that they find Halloween even *more* trying than Christmas.

Perhaps it is so dreadful because it signals something else. In Palo Alto, for example, during the two weeks that follow Halloween the schools go on minimum days, which means that all of the kids in the family are home most of the time—and at just about the same time that we are forced to start thinking about Thanksgiving and Christmas simply because all the decorations for those holidays start showing up everywhere.

At about the same time, newspaper articles start turning up about what stress-filled times the holidays are for most people. And every year, whether we read the articles or not, we anticipate the joy of the season, forgetting what we've read in the newspapers until we are faced with the work of preparing the feast and the trauma when it doesn't turn out to be absolutely wonderful. We make it through Thanksgiving, and the day after we are at the starting gate, racing to the stores and shopping centers to begin our Christmas shopping.

The next month finds us struggling with cards, writing Christmas letters, wrapping our presents, mailing packages, doing our special holiday cooking, and decorating our houses—complaining either outwardly or inwardly all the way, while holding out hope that this year will be better than last. When we get down to the wire—the week before Christmas—the kids are home from school for "winter vacation"; the weather is usually terrible, so they are underfoot.

And when mother holds down a full-time job, it's even worse. It is especially worse if the Christmas preparations are tossed into her lap. If she has children old enough to go to school but too young to stay home by themselves unless there is a full-time housekeeper, she has to reshuffle the child-care arrangements (as she does during other school breaks) and at a time when she is especially busy. I recall those days most vividly: shopping during my lunch hour, during snatches after work, and on Saturdays when the crowds were at their very worst; addressing cards and wrapping packages late at night when I should have been in bed—and absolutely hating every minute of it. Happy Holidays!

While we stretch our budgets to buy gifts for people who may neither need nor want them—"Here's an electric tie-rack for Uncle Harold"—we set ourselves up for exhaustion, crisis, and disappointment. Not only is there a tendency for parents to become more exasperated with their children than usual and the endless number of chores that "must be done," this is a time when more bitter battles between husbands and wives occur than at any other.

As is true with Thanksgiving, we all have the tendency to remember the holiday seasons of our childhood as being more joyous than they actually were, and each year seems to bring greater disappointment when compared to our fading memories of the good old days. To make matters worse for some of us, this is a time when we are likely to miss lost loved ones the most.

Then, even if the season does turn out to be joyous after all, there is nearly always a letdown as we bid good-bye to a familiar year we've lived through, noting that still another year of our lives has passed so very quickly.

To deal with it all, expectations must first be put in perspective—do not expect a stress-filled time to bring you joy just because the advertisers tell you it will. Christmas is a time when your children beg you for the toys they see advertised on TV, and you buy the toys only to see that minutes after they tear off the wrapping paper, they are bored with them. Expect that—*that's real.*

After the expectations are more in line with reality, look at some ways you can cut down on the actual work involved. Everyone tells you to shop early. If you must shop, I agree. But also let your fingers do some of the walking for you. Most department stores send out catalogs, so I recommend ordering as much as you can either by phone or mail—shopping can be dangerous, as any veteran who has been elbowed in the sides many times will tell you.

And speaking of mail, there is no valid reason for you to stand in line at the post office to mail a package when you can get a store to mail it for you. Virtually every major department store will send a package anywhere.

But then there are the Christmas cards. We don't send them anymore—oh, occasionally, we send a few, but we've noticed that most people would prefer not to send obligatory Christmas cards, and someone has got to take the initiative. This year, let it be you. If you and/or your husband are in business and are convinced that Christmas cards will enhance it, you should know that I'm not the only one who doesn't find receiving a Christmas card from a mortuary a reason to patronize the establishment that sends it.

Food. Why stuff a turkey or a goose when you can have a perfectly traditional Christmas with a beef roast that neither requires the cook to rise at the crack of dawn to stuff it, nor requires basting and worrying about when it will be done. And you can buy your pies from the bakery—unless you adore making them yourself.

However, the best Christmas in my memory was the one we didn't celebrate. We chose this time to take our vacation. We went to Mexico, where Christmas is celebrated not so much with exchanges of gifts and manufactured decorations, but with singing and dancing and homemade decorations put up shortly before the festivities start. Our children were eight and nine at the time and we worried that they would be disappointed at not having a traditional Christmas at home with a tree and presents. But as we were getting ready to come home, we asked them how they felt. Lisa said that the trip was the best present we'd ever given her, and Adam, who was especially impressed with the spontaneity he saw, said, "It gave me a spirit." We had run away from Christmas that year because there were two empty chairs we could not face—my parents would not be with us, again, and the year before their absence had hurt so very much. But even though time has worn down the grief we felt, whenever we can afford to, we will run away again.

Finally, my husband and I so fully recognize that the holidays are trying that every December 1 we declare a "just-in-case-we-need-it- truce." We agree that no matter what, we will not fight with each other over *anything*. When we disagree, we say, "Save it for January." Admittedly, it took time to recognize why December was the only time we ever discussed divorce in our household, and it took time to get into the habit of putting off our arguments for a month or so.

Maternal Fatigue

It goes without saying that fatigue is an integral part of mothering young children. There may be some question about whether the mother who holds down a full-time job outside the home is more or less subject to fatigue than the woman who stays home all day. There is no one answer simply because that would depend on what sort of support systems are available or lacking, how many preschoolers there are, how many other children, how demanding they all might be, and what sort of job mother might have. For example, a mother of an only child who has a supportive husband, whether she works or not, is obviously less subject to being worn down than the mother of three, whether or not she works. I know mothers of several children who work full time, have housekeepers, and are married to men who really do try to share some of the burdens, and they are far less subject to exhaustion than their counterparts who stay home all day and function in the traditional role. I also know working mothers of one or two children who don't have that sort of help and are utterly exhausted most of the time. And I know a mother of one whose job is so demanding that there's hardly anything left of her at the end of her routine ten- or eleven-hour days at the office.

Having said that, I think it is fair to say that there are two fundamental differences between working mothers and housewives that may set them apart when it comes to fatigue and the way they respond to their children. Or, quite possibly these differences may serve to show that trade-offs exist no matter how a mother spends her day. On the one hand, a working mother is in a pressure cooker from the time she gets up in the morning. Every minute is bespoke for *something*. There is little time to sit and rest and think or recharge the batteries. But as exhausted as a working mother may become, as filled with dread at moving from one job to the next, when she walks into the house at night, the time she has to deal with her children isn't in addition to having already spent ten or more hours with them. Thus, the mother who is home is more apt to feel resentment toward the children if they are seen as the primary reason for her fatigue. Familiarity *does* breed contempt.

No matter what your mothering role, when fatigue hits, all the rules fly out the window. Try telling an exhausted working mother, "It's better for mothers to work because it's the quality of time and not the quantity you spend with your children that counts," when all that greets her is zero quality in the first ten minutes after a trying day at the office. Or, try telling a mother of preschoolers that she's having an easier time because she doesn't have to work, when she's totally drained from chasing kids around all day. Neither will hear you.

Fatigue can be insidious, in that you aren't always aware of it. It sometimes masquerades as energy. One woman, for example, had reached the end of her tether and said she was ready to vigorously spank every bottom in sight: "I was hyper—I was all wired up with energy and anger. A friend came by and when she saw the state I was in, she offered to take my boys off my hands for a few hours. Well, after they left, I sat down for a few minutes to think about what to do with this sudden windfall of time. I fell asleep! I slept until my friend brought the kids back four hours later. I was tired and didn't even know it."

Be aware that angry or negative feelings can be more acute when you are tired. And also be aware that fatigue isn't always apparent to the one experiencing it.

Moving

I wish that management-level executives who make such decisions in large corporations were aware of the hell that transferring families all over the map can play—or if they *are* aware, that they would care more about the welfare of the families of their employees. Children suffer tremendously from relocation for the obvious reason that they leave their friends behind, and those who are already in school have to start all over in a new school and make adjustments similar to those they made during the first scary days when they started school. But no one suffers more than mother. A move means more work, more stress, coping with the stress of her children, and being cut off from her friends and quite possibly her own family—it may signal the end of any support system she might have developed. This is a serious danger zone, and a mother can go completely to pieces and wind up taking it all out on her children, when she really is seething over having been moved about like a chess piece on a board and having her life turned upside down.

Meanwhile, fathers don't suffer nearly so much because they have their work, outside contacts, and many opportunities to make new friends—sometimes they are even transferred with old friends from work. Which, of course, is why corporate executives don't recognize the problem when they transfer employees; I shouldn't have to point out, that at that level most are not mothers.

Money

An obvious danger zone exists when the family budget is tight and lack of money prevents parents from enjoying some time together away from their young children. Less obvious is the difference in attitude a parent can have toward a child's behavior when finances are shaky. For example, a parent's reaction to a child breaking something that has to be replaced, such as a window, at a time when the parent doesn't know where the money to pay for it will come from is bound to be different from the reaction of a parent whose affluence is such that replacing a window is a trivial matter.

And something that few people talk about is the way some parents react when their children accidentally hurt themselves. Concern for a child's welfare can deteriorate into resentment when this emergency visit, caused by a child doing something he or she knew he wasn't supposed to do, wound up costing another unaffordable $50 or so at the doctor's office.

To some people money means time. The parents who can easily afford household help, for example, have less reason to be perturbed when small children make messes than do the parents who do all their own chores. And the parents who translate the replacement of a broken window into giving up the child care it could have paid for can easily feel resentment at being denied some needed relief from parenting.

Murphy's Law

Everyone at one time or another experiences a day when Murphy's Law—that if anything can go wrong it will—prevails. The baby gets sick and cries through the night, leaving you exhausted; the washing machine goes out; the water heater blows; the car won't start; your checks bounce; you have a fight with your husband; your three-year-old picks this time to go into the yard of the fastidious childless couple next door and tears up their prize tulips; you notice your menstrual period is three days' late, and the relative you detest more than any other decides to come by and bother you for an hour or so.

A day like this is so unbearable that the only alternative a mother may feel she has is either to commit herself to a mental institution, run away from home, or lock herself in the bathroom. But she can't do any of these things because she must do all of her chores and take care of the children.

The mother who is at home with her children all day quite likely spends the day trying to make it take a different turn, but she walks around like an explosion waiting to happen.

When we are geared to finding solutions, it is difficult to give up searching and hoping, even on a day that is impossible. But there are times when I think it's important to recognize that there is absolutely nothing that can be done. And to continue to battle these strange forces will most likely lead to more problems and an endless amount of frustration and anger. Accepting a day when everything goes wrong instead of resisting may well be the only way to save any part of it and preserve your sanity.

I have, on several occasions, recognized that there was nothing whatsoever I could do to change the way a particular day was going, so I did absolutely nothing. And while I may not have accomplished anything, I didn't do any further damage. And I discovered something along the way. That if what I set out to accomplish one day doesn't get done—unless it is a matter of life or death, in which case I'll dial 911—it doesn't matter. Nothing terrible happens if I don't get all the household chores done, if I don't drive the children to wherever it is they think they must go, if I don't get the laundry done or cancel a routine dental or medical appointment. I've learned that nobody ever dies from dirty underwear, and that malnutrition won't set in if I don't cook dinner on a bad day—there *are* restaurants, and a hamburger from McDonald's tastes good once in a while. Actually, it tastes better with the knowledge that making it didn't add to the mess in the kitchen—in fact, on a bad day, the chances are if you made an attempt to cook, the kitchen would go up in a grease fire.

But the point to remember is that on the bad days, young children are moving targets—it is all too easy to vent your wrath and frustration in their direction.

School Days

If you have very young children, something to cling to when the going gets rough is that some of the pressures you are now feeling start to ease up when the children go away part of the time. That is, when they go off to school. However, if you make the mistake of thinking that from here on, it's all smooth sailing, you're asking to be disappointed.

As is true in nearly all aspects of life, there are trade-offs at this stage. The positive changes that take place when your children go to school are that they will have become more self-reliant and less mischievous by this time, and during the school year you will have relief from parenting them at least part of most days. The other side of that is that they aren't gone that long, and when your first child starts school, this will be the first time that the mother who stays at home will struggle nearly *every day* to get a child dressed and out of the house at a specific time. As any working mother who does this routinely will testify, a child's dawdling is never so irritating as when you are racing against either the school bell or the time clock at work or both! You can find yourself in a situation where you really explode and hurl insults and then afterward are consumed with remorse. The only way I know to prevent most of the early-morning eruptions is to get up *early,* get the kids up *early,* and make them get dressed *before* they sit down to breakfast. Even then, know that one child will forget his lunch or snack or that all-important thing he or she was planning to take to show and tell, and you are late all the same.

There are some other pitfalls to having the children in school. Some new-to-the-school-system mothers say they are overwhelmed by all the little notes and forms their children bring home from teachers, school nurses, and PTA stalwarts, and all the phone calls they suddenly start receiving from people who want them to become active in the PTA or school projects.

Parent-teacher conferences can be terrifying and many mothers feel they are personally on the line when a teacher evaluates their children. Most teachers are fairly sympathetic to mothers, but there are just enough who aren't to make a mother's first experiences a living hell. The mother who is already feeling unsure of herself can be reduced to tears and agony by teachers who know just how to apply pressure, and she is also the mother who is most likely to believe a teacher's every word. Some teachers really do make mountains out of molehills, leading parents to believe that what may actually be normal behavior for a particular child at a particular stage of development is evidence of pathology. It is difficult for a parent, especially one on shaky ground, to assess either a problem or the *actual* expertise of a teacher or a school psychologist. It's even more difficult when these professionals confuse the issues by covering up the fact that they don't always know what they're talking about with a lot of pseudo-scientific jargon.

Finally, something else that seems to intimidate many parents I've talked to is that their meetings with teachers stir up old memories of *their* experiences when they themselves were children. As one mother put it, "For the first two years that my children were in school, every time I had to meet with a teacher or the principal, I found myself behaving as if *I* was six years old, back in school, and would be graded on my performance. I was the pupil again, the teacher was *my* teacher, and the principal, the principal of *my* school."

In the beginning, having the children in school *can* create a new danger zone for mothers—one that is damaging to their self-esteem. But if you are prepared for some of the negative aspects that may surface, you can mark this period as a time when all of the danger zones gradually become less hazardous to your mental health and less apt to set the stage for domestic explosions.

There isn't much a mother can do to change the weather if it has a negative effect on her, or alter the phase of the moon, or rearrange the holidays so that they fit in better with her particular schedule. And I cannot tell someone how to feel better when she feels terrible because her marriage is falling apart. But I am a firm believer in the idea that *forewarned is forearmed.* If we develop the facility for recognizing those times when we are apt to feel anger over trivia, or misdirect our anger to our children when we're really not mad at them at all, it helps us sort out those days from the normal danger zones and take special precautions to avert the worst.

4

How Sticking It to Mother
Became a National Pastime
(and How to Fight Back)

If you are confronted in the emergency room by a middle-aged person with a bruised ego, fractured psyche, or flattened pocketbook, oozing guilt from every orifice, be on your toes. You may be dealing with a battered parent.

It will do no good to report the case, and there is no known cure. Perhaps the best you can offer is the hope that that the symptoms will eventually abate, when the children have gained understanding by virtue of having become victims of the syndrome themselves.[1]

> Dr. Robert B. Howard
> Advice to fellow
> physicians

You are a working mother and have been up since five-thirty A.M. While getting ready for work you notice that your preschooler, up earlier even than you, has redecorated the bathroom wall with your lipstick. You tell yourself you'll just have to take care of it after work—maybe before you start dinner. Then, while you're making breakfast your husband discovers the lipstick, tells you about it, and asks why you can't control the child.

After you've dropped one child off at the sitter's and another one at school, you are sitting at your desk making a list of the errands you'll run during your lunch hour. Your husband, who leaves the house after you do, calls to tell you the cat crapped in the hall closet. You hang up, finish your list, and get started on the work you're being paid to do. The phone rings again. This time it's the school nurse. She wants to know why you haven't done anything about getting glasses for your daughter—she explains that weeks ago she sent home the notice informing you that Debbie flunked her eye test. Your initial panic gives way to a twinge of guilt for being neglectful.

The next day is Saturday. You've cleaned house and it is now four in the afternoon and the first time you've had a minute to yourself. You are about to take your shower. But first you sit down on the john, an act which activates both the telephone and the front doorbell. You hear a crash, the baby starts crying, and your other child is banging on the bathroom door yelling that she wants some Fritos.

You've been up since about six A.M. You started your day by feeding, changing, and cuddling the baby and putting him back in his crib for a morning nap. You made breakfast for the family, prodded your dawdling six-year-old to get into her clothes and down to the bus stop in time, have refereed one battle between her and the four-year-old, and have seen your husband off to work, promising to run the errands he asked you to run. With everyone who was going anywhere gone, you cleared away the breakfast dishes, tossed on your clothes, and are doing your housework with the four-year-old alternately following you around and getting into mischief. You've been at it for a while and have just started to tackle the toilet bowl. The four-year-old shows up, comes into the bathroom, and wants to know when you're going to fix his lunch, when you're going to take him to Disneyland, why you can't read him a story, and where he put his shoes. Before you can sort out the questions, he flings himself on the floor in a fit of rage, screaming, "WYNCHA EVER AN-SWER ME?" In a moment of self-pity you wonder why you are being punished for cleaning the toilet bowl.

After lunch, the four-year-old takes a nap. You are in the shower and the phone rings. It's your six-year-old's teacher. As you stand dripping and shivering, she wants to set up an appointment to discuss the possibility that your daughter's grades are slipping because she's "educationally handicapped."

Perhaps it's summer. You get up at around eight, see to breakfast, and take about six calls *from* kids *for* kids and two from neighborhood mothers. Between the calls, you persuade your five- and six-year-olds to eat the "yucky" food you've fixed. Then, because you've decided that the kids should have swimming lessons (in the winter it's dancing and music) to help build self-confidence through accomplishment, and for safety, you get dressed and prod them to get into their swimsuits.

The lesson starts at ten, but because of all the dawdling and squabbling you rarely get there on time. You remind the children to take a try at making their beds, remind them once again to get into their swimsuits, and pick up some towels—it would, of course, be easier and faster just to do everything yourself, but you're trying to teach self-reliance.

At about nine-thirty you get in the car, once again telling the children to bring some towels. A fight breaks out just before takeoff: "He touched me . . . She bugs me . . . He took my whacky packies . . . she stole my dime . . ." You head out into traffic with one child kicking the back of your seat and the other chattering incessantly. Cars turn in front of you, bikes zip out from nowhere, trucks nearly jackknife into you. Another fight breaks out. You pull over to the side of the road and tell the kids to knock it off or you'll punch them out. You say for the thousandth time, "Do you want me to wreck the damn car???" And then you tell them you won't budge until they settle down.

You sit on a hard bench with the other mothers and you mention to one—one whose children are older than yours—that you think you're about to crack up. She tells you, "En*joy* them now. It will get worse."

After the swim lesson, comes the dialogue:

"C'mon, let's go, kids."
"I don't wanna."
"I don't wanna neither."
"Get your towels and get in the car."
"Can we go to McDonald's?"
"No."
"I don't wanna go then."
"Can we go to Aunt Barbara's?"
"No, I have things to do."
"I wanna stay here and swim."
"Get in the car. *NOW!*"
"No."
"GET IN THE DAMN CAR BEFORE I START SCREAMING!"
"Hey, you don't hafta yell."
"You said a swear. I'm telling."

These are isolated incidents of *mild* parent battering. Taken one at a time, they don't cause much damage or leave lasting scars. But when daily life is a variation on such themes, the situation can best be described as chronic abuse, which does cause deterioration. And when other factors come into play, such as very active children and large doses of parental guilt that comes from the sense that everything we feel, say, and do is wrong and damaging to our children, then the situation is critical: it is then hardcore parent battering, which causes *serious* deterioration and leaves sad scars on the soul.

Compassionate experts are in a minority, as indicated in this excerpt from a report by Kenneth Keniston and the Carnegie Council on Children, which dealt with the American family under pressure:

Although the experts differ, they share one basic assumption: that parents alone are responsible for what becomes of their children . . .

Naturally, if parents are considered solely responsible . . . they must be held at fault if things go awry. It is easy to leap from here to the conclusion that children's problems are caused entirely by the irresponsibility, selfishness, and hedonism of their parents . . .[2]

It's All Your Fault, Mother

I have drawers full of research—my husband calls it masochism—about the thousands of ways we parents screw up our children. I pick up an article I've clipped on childhood alcoholism: it is called, *How Parents Fail*. I read two paragraphs and learn that even eight-year-olds can become alcoholics, and then I transiently wonder if I am driving my children to drink. I then think about the parents of a boy who tripped out on one of the intoxicants of the sixties—LSD. He was a young teenager, subject to peer pressure. He never recovered from a bad trip and neither did his pain-filled, guilt-ridden mother who remains convinced to this day that she failed her child.

I pick up an old column of Lee Salk's. Once again I read that children don't misbehave unless they have a reason: either they are getting too little attention or not getting the *right* kind of attention. Lee Salk flies across the room and I pick up a note sent to me by a psychologist friend. It seems that one researcher, J. H. Van den Berg, has considered the effects of early childhood trauma and maternal deprivation and thinks they may have been exaggerated; he suggests that this had led parents to be *overly* affectionate, thereby creating neuroses in their children. Damned if you do, damned if you don't.

The idea that if you're a mother you can't win triggers a memory from my early days at this job. Many years ago when my children were only two and three and I used to put them down for the night at about seven, I read an article that made me feel I was doing something monstrous. Even though the children always went right to sleep, I suffered a twinge as I read that a couple of experts felt that often parents put children to bed early to get rid of them, that the children *knew* this, and thus felt *rejected*. Ignoring that young children *do* need their rest, these "experts" ignored something equally as important— that perhaps putting preschoolers to bed at night when an exhausted parent has had *enough* is one of the better alternatives.

However, such a suggestion, *even now,* is unacceptable, for we are living in a child-centered, mother-diminishing culture, which ignores that parenthood can be a one-way ticket to an institution. Also ignored is the fact that always blaming mother and accusing her serves to fan the fire of her smoldering, silent anger. And when an angry mother is *already* embroiled in the genuine problems of daily living, she may be left with nothing more to give than contained indifference or rage.

Under some circumstances, this rage can easily be triggered into an explosion when a child does something as trivial as walking through the room at the wrong time. And I say *a* child advisedly. Although it is true that mothers' explosions may be generalized, and when they become angry they want to let everyone within range "have it," many mothers who have more than one child seem to direct their anger at one in particular. Sometimes the anger is actually caused by something the child does and is understandable. But at other times the anger is completely displaced—it is anger at herself, her husband, or life in general. And the child who turns out to be the target for it may be one she actually doesn't like very much (which, of course, she feels guilty about), one who resembles her, one who reminds her of herself at some point in the past that she'd rather not think about, or one who resembles a relative she resents or dislikes. Or, perhaps the child was conceived or born at a particularly difficult time in her life. Then, of course, there could be a combination of factors involved when one child is seen differently from other children in the same family. For example, this excerpt from a fourteen-page letter one mother sent to me, for whom all of the stops had come out:

> *I am twenty-eight years old, married, have two beautiful girls, aged four and five years, and am hopelessly frustrated. I HATE BEING A MOTHER! I can't send my girls back and wouldn't if I could. My biggest problem is that my first child is next to perfect. She is easy to discipline, and I have NEVER felt resentful toward her. I thought one more child could only add to our happiness. The problem was that my second child was a very good, happy baby until she turned into a one-year-old. Whereas number one would play in her crib until she was two years old, number two was climbing out at thirteen months. We had to buy a harness to keep her in at night. That was only the beginning. She does what she wants when she wants to. She will do anything to defy me. I don't spank her anymore because a couple of times I almost hurt her . . . One time she broke one of my stack tables and I was so*

angry I took her three-foot inflatable bunny (a present from me) and stabbed it full of holes with my scissors, screaming "an eye for an eye." My husband fixed the table in ten minutes. My little girl never even cried over the destruction of the bunny. The only thing my act accomplished was my feeling that I'm cracking up.

From the day I brought my second child home, I felt guilty that my oldest one was going to feel left out or jealous (because everything I ever read on the subject warned of this possibility). She was always affectionate . . . It wasn't until our youngest one was one and a half that SHE started wanting love and affection. Now our five-year-old is a well-adjusted, happy child. Our four-year-old has been a monster since she was one and a half . . . she wets her pants, doesn't get along with other kids, and wants attention constantly. She asks for something and wants it ten seconds ago. She makes me a nervous wreck. Either I'm a bad mother or we just have bad chemistry.

I pray daily for patience, try to hold my feeling in, and hope I don't crack up (who would take care of the kids???). I feel it's my fault she's the way she is because my girls are sixteen months apart and my youngest one didn't get as much love and affection as my older one. But she was a happy baby and didn't seem to want affection.

It could easily be said that it is indeed this mother's fault that her youngest daughter is so much more difficult to handle than the older girl because her mother didn't give her enough attention from the start. But then, since the child eventually did demand attention, it could also be true that children *do* make their needs and desires known and this particular child didn't want much attention at first. Then this mother might actually dislike her second child for any one of the classic reasons I've already mentioned. Or, she could dislike her because she's obnoxious and dislikable—just as some *adults* are unpleasant, some children are, too, just because they are, and not necessarily because their mothers made them that way.

Ruling out all of the above, this particular child might be the target of her mother's wrath because she is one of those children who is, by nature, very active and would be difficult for *anyone* to deal with—the sort of child who makes a mother want to build a bonfire out of every child guidance book she has ever cracked.

The Active Child

Anyone who is a parent to a very active child does not need to be told how hard it is to cope, how frustrating it is, and how stupid and ineffectual you can feel when at the mercy of a tiny powerhouse. Or, how one can be overwhelmed with the urge to commit mayhem. And I'm not certain that those who haven't had the experience, even provided with a blow-by-blow description, can understand (and that would include experts who may offer suggestions for coping with them without having experienced them on a regular basis).

However . . . I would describe the very active child as one who is basically nonmalicious and one who moves faster than is believable. He or she is extremely curious and his determination, when he wants to do a particular thing, is so strong that he or she doesn't think about repercussions or what is forbidden. Like most children, he or she is immature, so he or she hasn't yet really grasped the idea of cause and effect. Often, if he is forbidden to do certain things, he'll forget that they are forbidden and do them on impulse. Sometimes even if he does know he will "get it," he decides that the pleasure of the doing is worth the risk of being flogged. When he gets to the point where he is able to remember the rules and abides by most of them, he is capable of dreaming up a whole new set of activities that ultimately will fall into the forbidden category—activities that his mother, Dr. Spock, Dr. Salk, and Dr. Bettelheim would never have imagined.

He is the boy, or she is the girl, who, forbidden to play with matches, sets fire to paper using a magnifying glass and then says, "But you didn't say I couldn't, you just told me about the matches." When you tell him he can't run his bike off a five-foot ramp, nor can he use any of the wood you've stored in the backyard for *anything,* he builds a *three*-foot ramp out of the leaves of your dining table. A mother ultimately ends up saying, "You cannot do anything without asking me first," and then worries that she's stifling creativity or being overprotective, having read somewhere of this danger. But she gets her answer when the child asks, "Can I go to the bathroom? Can I tie my shoe? Can I eat my dinner? Can I drink my milk? You said I couldn't do anything without asking you first. Can I go to bed?" When she is exhausted from all of the questions and play-acting, she might then rescind the blanket order and find herself back at square one.

Pediatricians frequently tell mothers that children really do want to please their parents. I think that active children want to please their parents, but they just don't wish to do so as passionately as all of the other more interesting things they can think of. They seem generally to have relatively little fear either of parental wrath or concern for their personal safety. They are the ones you read about who suffocate in abandoned refrigerators—they have been told *never* to do so, but they crawl in because their curiosity had been roused about what's in there that's forbidden and because they can't leave *anything* alone. Those who survive generally talk a lot. They want to know absolutely everything about everything. They can bombard all of a mother's senses from the time they walk and talk. And when they're not making noise, they're generally doing something terrible! Oddly enough, quite often they are especially delightful children they have so much personality—which adds to keeping mothers' emotions swinging dramatically back and forth. And often they are the world's most successful adults.

This child, if he or she is like my son, can nearly blind a mother with his or her charm one moment, and the next make her more angry than is healthy for anyone. It's not unusual for the mother of such a child to say something like, "If you get hit by a car and die, I'll kill you," as he maintains a climate of fear riding off ramps, climbing on roofs, and introducing new dimensions of anxiety and danger on a near-daily basis. You throw out all the rules with a child like this—especially the rules that say you shouldn't overdo your warnings and frighten your children. To get across to such a child that something is dangerous, you have to scare the devil out of him, and even then, he's probably going to do what he wants to do anyway. When he's quiet, it's either because he's setting fire to the garage or running a temperature of 105°.

How does a parent control a child like this? A child who, at age three, somehow manages to get his trike over a six-foot fence, climb over, then get on it and take off—only to be found by his distraught mother, riding down the middle of the train tracks? How does she control him when, just before he takes off on one of his outings, he puts water in the gas tank of her car so she can't go looking for him quickly—which is the only way you look for such children. What does she do when he's "napping" and he quietly climbs out of his bedroom window and somehow winds up on the roof? And what does she do when the same boy, now eight, launches a missile which lands on the roof of a neighbor's house, setting fire to it? What does she do when he's gone on a rampage and she remembers that someone told her how to throw water on him to shock him out of it, and she does, and one hour later when she walks out to empty the garbage he turns the garden hose on her?

Is there anything more a mother can do when she's warned, taken away all privileges time and again, yelled, and, against all expert advice, threatened him or tried to make him feel guilty? And has been consistent in all warnings and threats? Because all of these incidents have occurred, and because they represent only a tiny sampling of what I've heard about or experienced firsthand, I put these questions to a social worker whose specialty is child protection. Her answer?

"You beat the snot out of him."

Which is precisely what some mothers do, and which I emphatically don't recommend for the primary reason that "beating the snot out of him" would probably make you feel utterly terrible later on. And usually it isn't very effective. It should be noted, for the record, that psychologist Richard Bell tends to disagree with the reasoning of most experts concerning the cause and effect of severe punishment. He argues that "many studies claiming to show the effects of parents on children can just as well be interpreted as showing children's effects on parents. For instance, a study finding a correlation between severe punishment and children's aggressiveness is often taken to show that harsh discipline produces aggressive children; yet it could show instead that aggressive children evoke harsh child-rearing methods in their parents . . ."[3]

I agree. Especially where active children are concerned. My own gentle mother, who rarely (if ever) raised a hand to any of her four children once, jokingly—I think—suggested that I tie Adam to a tree. And believe me, there have been times when I thought that might be the only answer. And this is as good a place as any to say that I absolutely refuse to accept the blame for his inherent makeup. Adam is Adam. And my feelings about having such a son are, understandably I think, ambivalent. He has driven me mad, he has scared me more than any mother should ever be scared. And yet . . . he is one of the most fascinating human beings it ever has been my pleasure to know. I absolutely adore him—which is why he scares me, of course. He has a quick and curious mind, a zest for adventure, and a total love of life. However, I often feel that he needs at least five parents simply because the job of parenting a boy such as he is an enormous one.

Are the Experts Always Right?

One psychologist who writes a weekly column insists that the reason children suck their thumbs is that they don't get enough affection from their parents. I found that awfully hard to swallow given the number of well-loved thumb-sucking children I have known over the years. So I asked a speech therapist (who is also a psychologist) what he thought about this theory. He said that *nobody* knows exactly why children suck their thumbs. Because he has a program for breaking the habit, he's seen lots of thumb-suckers and he insists that virtually none of his clients are emotionally deprived.

And never forget that one psychologist published a study in *Human Behavior* magazine that showed that the reason why most mothers hold their babies in their left arms is so their babies will be close to their hearts. One could easily deduce from this conclusion that mothers who *don't* hold their babies in their left arms are social deviants, perhaps with emotional problems. But mothers themselves came to the rescue when they wrote to the magazine to say that the reason *they* held their children in their left arms was that they were right-handed—this left their right hands free to feed their babies or tend to whatever needed to be tended while holding them. Those who do otherwise, then, are not social deviants, after all, but simply left-handed.

I am not going to cite all of the misinformation that is authoritatively dispersed by psychologists—in itself, that would fill a volume. But one more I can't resist. One widely read psychologist insists that parents get upset when their children argue with them because they, the parents, feel that their authority is being threatened. I asked six mothers if they agreed. All six said that the reason they got upset when their children argued with them was that it was *annoying*—and they didn't like to be harassed.

Whether it is giving incorrect information or blaming parents, I think one of the reasons *some* experts have to find underlying reasons for everything, with the underlying reasons pointing to mother, is that this is a very handy explanation when they don't know what they're talking about.

When Belief in Theories Backfires

When we mothers *blame ourselves* for everything and put all our faith in fallible gurus, we can blow things out of all proportion. One mother who did this told me how she failed with her six-year-old, who steals. He took money from her purse and candy from the grocery story. She lectured him and took away his privileges, and he promised not to steal. After many episodes, they were coming home from the grocery store and the boy told her, "Mom, I feel so good—so much better because I don't steal anymore." His mother was proud and told him so.

That afternoon, when she was putting some clothes in his drawer, she found three candy bars and two packs of chewing gum. With a sinking heart, she realized that he'd taken these things while they were at the store together—just before he'd told her he'd reformed. After confronting her son, who told her he knows it's wrong to steal and he won't ever do it again, she went quietly into the living room and sat down and sobbed. Later she told me, "I don't know what to do. He lies and steals and I know it's because I'm doing something wrong. The experts say that's the only reason a child would do such a thing."

Dr. Spock would agree. While he notes that small children under the age of three take things that don't belong to them, and that isn't stealing because they don't have a sense of what belongs to them and what doesn't, when a child of six or older steals, it *means something*. What does it mean? "In most cases," writes Spock, "the child is unhappy and lonesome to some degree. He doesn't have a sufficiently warm relationship with his parents, or he doesn't feel completely successful with children his own age. (He may feel this way even though he is actually quite popular.)"

Now we get down to the nitty-gritty—the relationship with his parents: "I think the reason that stealing occurs more around seven is that the child at this age may be feeling particularly distant from his parents . . ." So, keen on parents always playing some role in childhood larceny, Dr. Spock contradicts his earlier assertion with respect to younger children with this: "A craving for more affection probably plays some part in stealing at all ages." Stick it to us!

But Spock doesn't leave it at that. He does have a solution to the problem. Under the heading of "What to Do for the Child Who Steals," he suggests, "It is time to think over whether the child needs more affection and approval at home, and help in making closer friendships outside."[4] The last time I saw this mother and this child, I would have thought a section in the book entitled, "What to Do for the *Mother* of a Child Who Steals" would have been appropriate. Her son, my son, and two other boys were happily playing with a train set—she was sitting at my kitchen table crying her heart out and talking about family counseling.

Is it even remotely possible that the reason a child might steal is that he wants something? Like that which he steals? And is there a chance that even if a six- or seven-year-old knows it's wrong to steal, *he is still too young to have developed the strong sense of morality necessary to help him resist the temptations that are tantalizingly displayed before him?* Isn't it possible, since so many children this age steal, that it will all sink in with the passage of time?

I am not going to debate Spock as to lack of affection being a motivating factor in *extreme* cases. In fact, I went all through school with a girl who drove all of her friends to distraction with her shoplifting. This girl had not just been denied affection but had suffered severe beatings at the hands of her mother and stepfather when she didn't perform perfectly in every superficial arena. In addition to being a thief, she was a pathological liar and, when she hit her teens, sexually promiscuous. I think that to use this poor, abused girl as a model that might apply to all children who steal would be absurd.

But then, many experts use extreme models to determine what may underlie the behavior of average children; in particular, psychologists who draw on what they learn from working with people who are seriously disturbed—even institutionalized. While it is true that much can be learned that way, and even applied to the general public, it may also be true that much that is applied doesn't apply at all. And I think there is a distinct possibility that a conscientious and once relatively stable parent can wind up reading *far too much* into some situations.

You can apply this to other behavior problems, so let's take the stealing example and look at it through the eyes of that poor, distraught mother. Stealing and lying are serious offenses to her, so already she's upset. She has to deal with the disciplinary aspects while she deals with the anger and resentment she may be feeling toward her child. Convinced that she is to blame because she hasn't given her child enough affection—for all we know she lavishes it on him—she feels guilty about that. And she's got to remedy the problem by being more affectionate and more approving. But she doesn't feel like it because she isn't feeling very affectionate and approving. Making matters worse is the possibility that if she gives approval the boy may get the message that stealing isn't so bad after all. On the other hand, if she forces herself to be affectionate when she feels otherwise, her child might pick up her bad vibes, or, God forbid, get one of those famous "double messages" that communication experts are always going on about.

At this point she's so overwhelmed she doesn't know what to think, feel, or do. The problem has turned into a nightmare because it has so many components. If she were not in such an emotional state she could look at stealing another way: even Spock points out that many six-year-olds steal at one time or another, and that should tell her something—like it might be a phase. It is serious, it should never be condoned or ignored, and the culprit should be made to return the contraband and be reminded (repeatedly) that stealing is wrong. It is natural for a mother to feel ashamed of her child—and fearful and angry—but neither the stealing, her feelings, nor whatever may have motivated the child is cause for serious alarm and self-castigation.

Another mother, who got carried away with the idea that something she had or hadn't done was responsible for a problem her six-year-old son was having, recounted their experiences when the boy went through a period of seeming regression in his bowel habits, which resulted in his having frequent accidents. This mother's initial reaction wasn't really all that unusual. She found swishing his shorts in the toilet most distasteful, and she was embarrassed when other people criticized her poor training of her child.

When this mother delved a bit deeper and applied a little psychology to the problem, she saw clearly what was going on: the child was behaving this way to get her attention, and so her logical conclusion was that she wasn't giving him enough of it. The answer then was to give him lots of love generally and to totally ignore this attention-getting device of his. When he saw that he was loved, and, further, that he couldn't get a rise out of his mother by messing his pants, he'd stop.

A month of loving and ignoring went by and nothing changed. Finally, all of his mother's "indifference" and forced affection burned themselves out. She became enraged and told him she knew he was doing this to bug her and she wasn't going to put up with it. Alternately she wondered what she as a mother was doing that was *so wrong* that her child would behave this way. Back and forth she went. Soon it was beatings and remorse, sandwiched in between extreme patience. The problem reached such large dimensions that this mother became consumed by it. Finally, in desperation, she called the pediatrician and took her child in for an examination. By this time she was sure that her son was psychotic and equally sure that it was all her fault.

As it turned out, her son had a *not uncommon physical problem* that was corrected with medication. The child's stools were especially large, causing his movements to be painful, so when he would get the urge to go, he'd become frightened and hold it. Little by little, he'd pass pieces of his bowel movements, thus the many small "accidents" that occurred throughout the day. The child, embarrassed and afraid of what was happening to him, didn't know how to express his fears to his mother and was suffering from physical discomfort—on top of which ultimately had been added his mother's wrath. Imagine this woman's remorse when she found out what she had put her child through! And all because of the false assumption that *she* was responsible for his behavior.

It does give one pause, now doesn't it? Incidents such as this strongly suggest that we might find that some of the problems with children are simply what they appear to be and not manifestations of more sinister psychological underpinnings. I think that it is significant that when we mothers doubt ourselves it very often leads to our doubting our children. That is, if we believe that what we are doing is responsible for the behavior of our children, then a component of that belief is that our children are intentionally misbehaving. Such an idea can keep us from giving our children the benefit of the doubt, which we might be more naturally inclined to do were we not generally led to believe that children have ulterior motives, that they are willful instead of simply immature, when they behave in ways that run counter to our values.

Furthermore, when the mother, convinced that she is the cause of all her children's problems, verbalizes this feeling with "I'm not a good mother," or, "Where did I go wrong?" how does a *child* feel when he or she hears such a statement? When my children were young, they responded to my put-downs of myself with either tears or anger. One day, a couple of years ago, I asked Lisa why that bothered them so much. She said, "When you say you're not a good mother that means I'm not a good girl because good mothers have good children." That is *one* "Why" I wish I'd asked *years* ago. I now know that when I feel like a dismal failure as a mother and give voice to that view, my children take that to mean that I'm disappointed in them *as people*—that they fall short of the mark, that they are inadequate. In other words, I can only be a failure as a mother if they are failures as children. I hope all experts who say they are concerned with a child's self-esteem will think about that the next time they lay a guilt trip on mothers.

Why We Ask Why and Why It's Not Such a Hot Idea

You do not have to reach for profound reasons when Stevie cuts up the draperies. *Why* is irrelevant. Take the scissors out of his hands and say loudly, so he will *hear* you, "DON'T CUT THE DRAPERIES!"

When you are tempted to ask your child why he does something or other, think about this: previous generations of parents didn't ask their kids *why* when the kids got out of line; they just took it to mean that kids were ornery sometimes. But *we* ask why. Why? Because we modern mothers have been conditioned by psychologists and other child-guidance experts *always* to look for underlying motives for a particular acceptable behavior—reasons *that make parents and not children* themselves responsible. And, of course, because now we are into "communicating," we ask, "Why did you do that?" Sharrol Munce Blakely, former director of California's Office of Child Abuse, says that the biggest mistake parents make when their children misbehave is to ask that question. Why? Because, she says, children usually don't *know* why they do certain things, so either they don't answer when asked, or they lie. And parents, already upset, see either the silence or the manufactured reason as an act of defiance, on top of other acts that have already made them angry, and this can lead to violence. In the extreme, Ms. Blakely told me, it can lead to the sort of situational child abuse* that can result in serious physical injury.

How Sticking It to Mothers Became the National Pastime and How that Is Destroying Family Life

There was a time when American culture truly extolled the virtues of mothers. Mothers were the backbone of the Republic, respected and admired for the difficult, clearly delineated jobs they had to do. Then came the shift, and the culture turned to extolling the virtues of mother*hood* to such an extent that those who chose the role or had it thrust upon them were considered to have been handed a piece of cake. The importance of mothers diminished as children became all-important.

It is really rather ironic that when second-class citizenship for women was an institution, officially sanctioned by denying women the vote, mother herself was more honored and re-spected than she is today. The regard for her importance was expressed in such sentiments as "The hand that rocks the cradle will rule the world." In the days of Margaret Sanger, mother-hood was thought to be a cross to bear and the woman who bore it to be valiant, courageous, and wise. Presidents and soldiers honored and respected their mothers until the merger of Freud-ian theory, technology, and the imagery of Madison Avenue gained strength and got a foothold in the culture, setting the

*Situational child abuse is that which occurs when environmental pressures and parental stress build up to such an extent that if a crisis occurs (either major or trivial) a parent temporarily loses control.

stage for putting mother down for the job she does. As E. L. Doctorow said in *Ragtime,* Harry Houdini was probably the last man ever to be in love with his mother, thanks to Sigmund Freud.

When I was a small child you were taught to respect your mother because she was your mother. Today's children seem to "honor thy mother" only if she *earns* their respect, and it is hard for her to do that when she is universally thought to be the source of all of her children's emotional ills. And I think this tendency starts at younger ages than many people think. When my son, for example, was six years old and he'd have a bad day at school, he'd come home and say to me, "It's *your* fault." Now, where did he get that idea?

You can watch the shift from mother to child take place when you look at the way pregnant women are treated. They are truly honored because thay are carrying precious cargo. They are fussed over, told to rest, eat well, stay out of drafts, and given seats on crowded buses. But once the baby arrives, they are told to get to the back of the bus traveling on life's highway, forget about their own journey, and focus on making that of the child the best it can possibly be.

And well she can devote all of her attention to her child now that she's been tossed a few appliances and other modern conveniences which leave her free to do so. The *work* has gone out of motherhood is the message. That's about as sensible as saying that now that the President of the United States has a telephone and an airplane, running the country should be a snap.

When supermother totally embraces the role and sees her entire worth as a human being in how expertly she raises her children, she either can become so worn out that she has no love left to give, or invest so much of herself in her children that she feels she *owns* them, having paid the going price. I think now of conversations I have had with young adults who complain that their mothers won't stop trying to run their lives; in particular, young women who say that their mothers cannot accept their life-style choices if they are different from those of their mothers, and young men who say that their mothers pressure them to go to college and make something of themselves, so that they reflect well on the family. You cannot blame mothers for continuing to mother when they have been intensely doing that for so long. Nor can you blame them for being possessive or feeling that they have a say in their adult children's lives, particularly if you acknowledge that after virtually negating their own lives that's a natural way to feel.

Conflicts, however, start earlier in the relationship between a supermother and her child. What if, after all of her efforts, she does not have a superchild who reflects well on her?

Another way the circle closes is when Freud's prophecies come true and the adult child, male or female, winds up on some shrink's couch with a complaint that boils down to: "My mother messed up trying to be perfect because you guys made her afraid not to be and now it's her fault that *I'm* all messed up." If I were truly paranoid, I'd suggest that the shrinks, following the lead set down by their "father," have conspired with Madison Avenue to make sure they have plenty of business for generations to come. And such a business!

What makes all of this even crazier is that every once in a while there is a "security leak," and a study surfaces that shows that except in *extreme cases*, where, for example, parents are truly psychotic, the average parent has very little negative influence on a child's life, and that, in fact, there are far too many other influences beyond the reach of a parent that are determining factors. Psychologist Arlene Skolnick, of the University of California at Berkeley, uncovered a whole batch of these studies and, no doubt to the chagrin of experts everywhere, published them in *Psychology Today*. Dr. Skolnick's conclusions not only are fascinating but should be reproduced by every mother and taped to the door of the refrigerator:

... Most child-care advice assumes that if parents administer the proper prescriptions, the child will develop as planned. It places exaggerated faith not only in the perfectibility of the children and their parents, but in the infallibility of the particular child-rearing technique as well. But increasing evidence suggests that parents simply do not have much control over their children's development; too many other factors are influencing it.

Popular and professional knowledge does not seem to have made parenting easier. On the contrary, the insights and guidelines provided by the experts seem to have made parents more anxious. Since modern child-rearing literature asserts that parents can do irreparable harm to their children's social and emotional development, modern parents must examine their words and actions for a significance that parents in the past had never imagined. Besides, psychological experts disagree among themselves. Not only have they been divided into competing schools, but they also have repeatedly shifted their emphasis from one developmental goal to another, from one technique to another.[5]

Fighting Back

I guess every culture needs a scapegoat—some class of citizen alternately blamed for all ills, neglected, or abused. In America, one scapegoat is mother, with the purge being led by those who study and judge her performance while sweeping aside her humanness. And as history shows, those who lead the pogroms against one group or another never develop the conscience to end the persecution—it is always those who are being persecuted who must rise up and say "Enough!" and fight back.

To do that first requires that we unlearn much that we have

learned and fully realize that for the most part parents have to fly by the seats of their pants. Ironically, we have all been brainwashed with so much instruction that we almost need a guide to tell us *how* to do just that. And I just happen to have one:

- Do not read or listen to words that make you feel guilty.

- Trust your better instincts; that is, those not rooted in vengeance or spite.

  Understand that you know more than you think you do—that for centuries women have raised children with love, common sense, and concern for their welfare and have been, for the most part, highly successful mothers.

- At least initially, accept situations and behaviors at face value; for example, if a child flings himself on the floor in a fit of rage, don't automatically assume that it's because of something you are or aren't doing. Consider instead that the child might be frustrated over something that has nothing whatsoever to do with you. Naturally, if you've just told him, "No, you can't have a cookie," his fit *does* have something to do with you, but I wouldn't worry about it. Do not look for hidden meanings for your child's every act—if you revitalize your instincts, your instincts will tell you when to do so.

- Don't try to make mutually exclusive ideas work for you; for example, when there's a common belief that two-year-olds are obstinate, and you have seen for yourself that they are, don't try to apply the common belief that you can reason with all children when, in fact, if you think about it you know that's not true.

- When you are worried about a child's behavior at a particular stage of that child's development, compare notes with other (honest) mothers.

- When in doubt—when you feel that you *cannot* trust your instincts, and really do need some expert advice in anything from feeding to dealing with a troublesome seven-year-old— consult your pediatrician, state your problems as honestly as possible, and ask for help, not just for your child but for *you.*

It is this last point that I feel is critical. While we must come to realize that we parents must rely heavily on our instincts and common sense to pull us through the job of parenting, I feel very strongly that we ought to use our pediatricians, one invaluable resource that most of us have access to and probably under-use. Ever since I discovered that our pediatrician was a human being, whenever I've had a problem I couldn't work out I've talked it over with him. I first had to get past the idea that it was important for him to approve of me totally as a mother— to get rid of the notion that every quarter he'd send me a report card that would show how miserably I was failing. I don't pay him for approval—I pay him for the expertise that comes from his dealing with children on a daily basis and being knowledgeable about the two I bring into his office. It is really silly to worry about what he will think of me, in view of the fact that he has, like most practicing physicians, seen and heard just about everything. He's not likely to be shocked when I say, "That child drives me bats and I could kill her with my bare hands." And, oh, it feels so good to say that sometimes.

I strongly urge mothers not only to state the problem of the moment to their children's doctors but to really explain what it's doing to *them,* the mothers. And ask for help. (Our doctor told me on more than one occasion when the children were small that I should take some time off.) Sure, a pediatrician's primary concern is for the welfare of his young patients, but he must know, or will learn it at some point, that parents need help and understanding, and most realize that the best way they can insure loving care for their patients is to provide those responsible for that care with the support and understanding they need. And those pediatricians who haven't realized it yet will get the message if enough mothers convey it often enough.

Another very good reason to consult a pediatrician when a child is driving you up the wall is that there may be some physical or neurological reason for the particular problem. Whether that is the case or whether your child is just being a child can best be determined by a competent pediatrician who *knows* the child.

If increasing numbers of mothers would turn to their children's doctors when they need help for themselves, we might just get a minor revolution off the ground. We might, through our pediatricians, popularize the idea that mothers are people too, which could lead to a new crusade to prevent psychological mother-battering. And somewhere along the line maybe those child-guidance experts and other critical members of our culture who are guilty of contributing to the emotional abuse of mothers would learn one of the basics—that if mothers are neglected and psychologically and socially abused, there's a good chance their children will be psychologically—and even physically—abused as well.

But, of course, the specialists who have helped to shape and reinforce prevailing biases toward mothers need first to look at the absurd paradox they have created: that, on the one hand, a mother is to blame for all her children's acts of misbehavior and every emotional problem they have ever had, presently have, or will have at some future date, and hence has enormous power; and on the other hand, because she herself is unimportant and only a mere instrument whose sole purpose is to see to her children's needs, she herself is nothing.

5

Recognizing and Expressing Secret Anger: To Spank or Not to Spank

It's taken me several years to come to terms with what I've been handed. A bright, healthy little boy who is affectionate and funny. But one who has nearly driven me out of my mind and caused me to become paranoid that he will never, because of his wildness, reach the age of twenty.

What really makes me feel that I'm crazy is that as much as I love this child and fear for his physical safety, there are times when I want to beat him within an inch of his life just to get even with him for damaging my marriage, breaking my things, and putting me through so much mental anguish.

Because of this I don't hit him anymore—that has never been an answer for my problems. I will just do the very best I can, try to be mature about it, and fervently hope that it all works out.

Brian's mother

The main purpose of spanking, although most parents don't like to admit it, is to relieve the parent's frustration. All of us need to do this from time to time when our kids get on our nerves.

. . . We get fed up when our kids misbehave and we lose our cool and swat them. But that's nothing to feel guilty about. We feel better and they feel better. The air is cleared.

Fitzhugh Dodson
HOW TO PARENT

In sifting through most of the popular child-guidance literature, it becomes clear that spanking is seen by most experts as
an integral part of parenting. Fitzhugh Dodson, for example,
while not endorsing the outright flogging of children, has much
to say on the subject. In *How to Parent*, he starts by pointing out
that you don't calmly tell a child who runs in front of a car not
to do it again, but instead reinforce this command with a few
healthy whacks. And he continues with, "I believe it is impossible to raise children effectively—particularly aggressive,
forceful boys—without spanking them." Saying that he has
never met a parent who does not get angry and that there are
times when we can smoothly handle the most difficult of our
offspring, he acknowledges that "there are other times when
the slightest annoying thing a child does is enough to set us
roaring at him."[1]

And both he and Benjamin Spock disagree with the old saying, "Never strike a child in anger." Dodson says that he believes that is psychologically poor advice and suggests exactly
the opposite: "Never strike a child *except* in anger. A child can
understand very well when you strike him in anger. He knows
you are mad at him and he understands why." What he can't
understand is hearing when he misbehaves that his father will
deal with him when he gets home. "That's the kind of cold-
blooded spanking a child cannot either understand or forgive
. . . Spank your child only when you are furious at him and feel
like letting him have it right then." Along the same lines, Spock
says, "You sometimes hear it recommended that you never spank
a child in anger but wait until you have cooled off. That seems
unnatural. It takes a pretty grim parent to whip a child when
the anger is gone."[2]

And yet—even with the sanctions from these two very well-
known experts (and many others)—there are many parents who
don't spank even when a child seems to be begging a parent to

take some sort of drastic action. Some parents don't simply because they don't discipline their children at all. Other parents don't because they are uncomfortable about hitting another person. And then there are some parents who don't spank their children because, at least for themselves, they subscribe to the view of those who say you should "never spank a child in anger."

In explaining why this is her rule, one mother told me, "When I'm really mad—I mean *mad*—at my daughter, nothing could make me hit her—one slap and I'd be done for because it wouldn't end there." Another said, "When my two-year-old drives me to despair, I keep my hands held tightly behind my back for fear of what I might do if I start using them." "There is a fine line between discipline and child abuse," said a father of three boys. "And there are times when I know if I start hitting, I'll just keep hitting, so at our house, we don't hit."

I have run from my kitchen in the heat of the battles that occur when the pots are simmering on the stove and the energetic juices of my children have brought me to the boiling point. I can't tell you precisely why, but I have known that if, at such a time, I were to give in to a nearly irresistible impulse to hit, it wouldn't stop with a mere spanking or a simple, conclusive slap.

The one thing shared by angry parents, who feel like hitting but do not, is the absolute knowledge that a spanking, initiated at the wrong moment—and possibly directed toward the most generally annoying child in the family, might turn into a beating. Some know this from experience, others just know it instinctively.

The Storehouse of Unresolved Anger

I think this angry experience, and what causes the furies to be unleashed and go out of control, can be compared to what happens in therapy groups where clients work through feelings of hostility by hitting a pillow either with fists or encounterbats. After the group leader tells a participant that it is okay to feel anger and encourages its expression, he or she may then suggest pretending that the pillow is the person for whom some present or past anger exists. I watched one woman take on the pillow. As she mentally returned to the angry-making occasion she really started to hit. The more she called the pillow "Ralph," the person toward whom she felt some unexplained anger, the angrier she became, hitting harder and harder and with more frequency. The first few angry hits triggered rage that she, just minutes before, wasn't consciously aware she was carrying around. When her anger subsided, the pillow was completely flattened out. It was only a pillow, of course, but I doubt that she would have behaved any differently, once she really got into her rage, had it actually *been* Ralph.

Like parents who fear they will lose control, this woman had a storehouse of unresolved anger that she had not expressed at times when it would have been appropriate to do so. And parents who carry around these "storehouses" not only carry around *unexpressed* anger but quite probably *unacknowledged* anger as well. And they reach a point where all of it can be triggered by something very trivial. Thus, for example, when a mother becomes enraged because her four-year-old tips over a glass of milk, she may later explain that it was "the final straw." But what made it "the final straw" was her inability to recognize or respond to her feelings as other irritating or angry-making incidents occurred over a period of hours, days, weeks, or even months.

And obviously, the inability to recognize anger makes it impossible to understand what really causes it or its intensity. I think that frequently the reason a parent feels inordinate rage when a child does something wrong is that, in addition to carrying around a lot of anger, certain acts—even accidents—are seen as expressions of hostility. For example, I had just finished mopping the kitchen floor when my son came in, went to the refrigerator, took out a bottle of soda pop, carelessly opened it and spilled it all over the counter and the floor. If that wasn't an act of hostility, at the very least it was one that either discounted me or was purely inconsiderate—even though it was an accident. Isolated, such an incident isn't likely to cause much anger—and my awareness of how I genuinely felt helped me to keep my responses in perspective.

However, when one is not aware of the undercurrent, and such incidents are mixed up in a whole string of acts that demonstrate contempt or discounting as well as a lack of effectiveness, anger over a trivial transgression can be enormous.

When a child takes his mother's things and doesn't return them, not only does this cause her great inconvenience and hours of searching, say, for a pair of scissors so that she can perform a simple five-minute task, but at some level, she may feel that she is being intentionally attacked. And why not? Psychiatrist Theodore Isaac Rubin maintains that when people borrow things and do not return them, whether consciously or not, they are intentionally displaying hostility.[3]

The child who accidentally knocks over a glass of milk can create a full-scale problem for a mother if the glass breaks and scatters all over the room. And it may or may not have been an act of anger directed *toward* mother, but what it accomplished in a split second was to convey a sense of hostility, create an unpleasant cleanup job for her, quite likely foul up her schedule, and in the case of a freshly waxed floor, cancel out a previous effort and tell her that she doesn't count.

Now this mother, at some level of consciousness, registers this as a full-blown act of hostility. And when she feels what is a normal spurt of anger over being treated badly, when she comes from *pure emotion*, she's not likely to be patient and successfully dismiss what occurred because "he's only a child and didn't mean it." And even if she can do that at a conscious level, if her reaction is still unconscious, she hasn't really convinced herself. A four-star production of inordinate rage might have these components: anger over being the target of another person's wrath, anger over being discounted, guilt feelings over being angry at all, and self-flagellation for being petty.

And not only is it human to *feel anger*, but it is also human to *want revenge*. Like the woman who stabbed her child's plastic bunny, screaming "An eye for an eye," the mother who spanks a child for insulting her person isn't disciplining but instead is getting even. It is my guess that few mothers have failed to feel this way on some occasion. The situation can become particularly intense for the mother who finds herself being *blamed* for a situation caused by her child. An example that comes readily to mind is that of the woman whose husband berates her for "letting" the children mess up the house. If he is angry and disapproving—when she is *already* upset—is it not human for her to be furious with the children for "getting her into trouble?" And to want revenge?

The Buttoned-Lip Syndrome

I think that what lies back of a parent's inability to acknowledge, express, or understand anger is the prevailing cultural attitude that normal parents never are supposed to experience this emotion. And it is an attitude that is reinforced even by those experts who *do* acknowledge that parents have feelings. As Angela Barron McBride, author of *A Married Feminist*, notes,

. . . (such specialists) always manage to convey the impression that any negative feelings in a parent should last only as long as it takes to read the five-page chapter. Apparently, mothers can

become cross but not ferociously angry, glum but not morose,
grouchy and irritable but never truculent and caustic. It is al-
most as if the authors were worried that if they referred to a
particular emotion by the strongest adjective, they might unleash
hideous maternal furies and provide a license for violence.[4]

Perhaps these experts would worry less about providing "a
license for violence" if they realized that no matter what they
say, their words are bound to be overwhelmed by that which
truly does shape cultural values and beliefs: the mass media,
which daily reinforces the notion that children are always well
behaved and parental anger is nonexistent. When, for example,
was the last time you saw a really angry parent on television?
Even an *unhappy* one? When was the last time you saw a child
throw a tantrum, or a bowl of cereal across the room in a
commercial, situation comedy, or soap opera? When was the last
time you saw parental anger outside of a documentary on domestic violence?

The fact is, in the worlds created by advertisers and television
producers, all mothers are happy, cheerful, and serene, and all
of the children are well behaved and clean—except, of course,
for the ones who generate enough dirt to turn a detergent
commercial into a success story. Put simply, there is no place for
anger—real anger—in normal, well-scrubbed American homes.

However much one might disdain the idea, the media *does*
influence us rather dramatically. This fact has been substanti-
ated by sociologists such as Vance Packard, but probably more
telling is the fact that advertisers continue to spend billions of
dollars to promote their wares. And they sell maternal tran-
quility as an idea right along with every product advertised.

But switching brands isn't the same as adopting a false ideal
that cannot be reconciled with basic human emotions. And in

the final analysis, the claims that advertisers make about their products turn out to be far more honest than the subliminal message of familial bliss that is portrayed by actors who "live" in spotless, well-ordered "homes." In fairness, I don't think it is the intent of the media to convince people that family life is perfect and devoid of anger. But they do. And the image that is projected winds up being internalized by those of us who receive it.

After talking to dozens of other parents, I'm certain that I'm not alone in saying that very early I "knew" that it was "wrong" to feel anger toward a child. I developed what was frequently an unconscious (and unnatural) response to irritating situations with my children. But periodically, inordinate rage would push its way through the layers of my denial of its very existence and catch me by surprise. When this happened, I would become even angrier (trying not to, of course) at having been made to feel the way only maniacs, not loving mothers, might feel. Making the cycle most complete was that no matter what I did—whether I hit or walked away—I added to my angry storehouse a certain amount of guilt.

Anger cannot be denied nor wished away; unexpressed or unacknowledged it remains—and festers. And if the emotion is not dealt with, on every angry-making occasion, it is added to what Theodore Isaac Rubin calls one's "slush fund of anger." Of course, guilt over "wrong" feelings gets neatly tucked away too.

Ignoring for a moment the vicious cycle that can build, try to put the notion that mothers *don't* get angry together with Fitzhugh Dodson's and Benjamin Spock's acknowledgements that *they do*. Next, add these ingredients:

- Paul Wood and Bernard Schwartz's statement that "expressing this anger is important because parental emotions are essential cues that help a child realize that what has been said was meant."[5]

- Theodore Isaac Rubin's assertion that anger must be acknowledged and expressed or it will accumulate and become a poison.

- The widespread and growing idea that yelling, swearing at, or insulting a child when you are enraged is a form of emotional child abuse that can scar for life.

- To speak softly through clenched teeth is to send a double message to a child and is confusing, dishonest, and quite possibly emotionally abusive.

Now, stir well. This is what I, as a mother, come up with: I should never feel angry with my children, but if I do, that is perfectly normal or abnormal, depending upon the point of view of whatever I am reading or whoever I may be observing. If I don't acknowledge and express my anger, it will build up and I'll blow sky high. Thus, I should tell my children when I'm angry with them, fully expressing my feelings, but I should take great care that I do not hurt *their* feelings, demean them in any way, scare them, or insult them, lest I will abuse them emotionally and cripple them for life. However, if I don't express my emotions honestly, the children will (a) receive double messages, or (b) know precisely what's on my mind because they pick up parental vibes. Finally, none of the above should ever become a problem of any magnitude simply because if I'm at all competent, I will have precluded most angry-making situations by being able to maturely control my children with a look, the tone of my voice, or my body language of the moment.

It is at this point that I wonder just who or what causes some parents to go absolutely bananas. Even a saint could not sanely manage the above emotional juggling act. Of *course,* children are responsible for the anger of their parents—but would parents become quite so angry if they were not additionally confused and frustrated? They get it from all sides: "You should do, you should not do, you should feel, you should not feel, you should be, you should not be . . ."

So, let's be sensible. Anger is real, children and situations cause and trigger it; suppressing or denying it only increases its intensity. But getting rid of it for some parents is a trade-off. They get rid of *momentary* anger, and then feel guilty about *how* they got rid of it, and then those guilt feelings turn into resentment and go back into Dr. Rubin's slush fund. All of this convinces me that any parent who is fearful that one swat might give way to a severe spanking (and resultant guilt) is wise to trust those instincts. We know ourselves. And we know that if we lose control we might do damage to a child and/or feel absolutely miserable about it—we know this better than any child-guidance specialist, psychiatrist, or parental pundit on the face of the earth.

The Parent Most Likely to Lose Control

One of the best indicators of *how* violent a parent is apt to become is how he or she was treated as a child. It is an established fact that people generally, when dealing with their children, repeat the patterns they themselves learned as children. This is called imprinting; very early, from infancy, we are being taught to be parents. Thus, if you are a very angry and violent parent, an *honest* examination of the relationship you had with your own parents, stepparents, or guardians is in order.

If you were treated unfairly, cruelly, and in a manner that robbed you of your self-esteem, the chances are very great that you will, without intending to, treat a child that way. You walk around with a triple-edged sword hanging over your head: you are repeating learned patterns and you have a lot of unexpressed anger for your parents—or whoever treated you cruelly. And while most people have a high expectation of what children will do for them, those who have suffered or been deprived of affection as children have generally a much higher expectation than normal. I cannot help but think that any woman who has experienced a harsh childhood and has grown up with the expectation that marriage and motherhood would make her happy, might just say to herself when it doesn't, "When do I get mine? Don't I deserve happiness somewhere along the line?" And she may be especially angry at those people—her children—whom she may see as being wholly responsible for her current extreme unhappiness and disappointment. All on top of the fact, of course, that motherhood isn't exactly a piece of cake.

Any mother who recognizes herself in the paragraph above and wants to seek help will find that her local mental health association can point her in the right direction, as can a local parent hotline. The prospect of outside help is sometimes frightening—needlessly so, I think, since, generally speaking, those who work with troubled parents are compassionate and understanding. And it isn't necessary to give your name when making such inquiries.

Another suggestion, and one that comes from some parents who have done it, is to observe the way in which parents who are more easygoing than you are interact with their children. You're likely to notice that they seem to understand that a child is a child, and not simply a small adult—that a child needs more than he is capable of giving and that he cannot perform many tasks, or is clumsy, or doesn't have any feeling for time, simply because he has yet to reach a particular stage of physical and mental development.

Finally, the parent who mistreats a child because he or she is repeating a pattern is carrying around a sense of worthlessness—a feeling that if he or she had not been a bad child his or her parents wouldn't have treated him or her the way they did. It's good to remember that what your parents did probably didn't have anything to do with you—in any *real* sense—instead they were simply repeating a pattern *they* learned.

How to Channel Your "Mother" Emotions Successfully

There is something I think *all* parents ought to be reminded of when they really feel like letting their children have it. *Most people who hit their own children don't hit other people's children.* Not even when they really actively dislike them and are boiling mad at them. The difference between your children and someone else's, obviously, and most importantly, is that you can get away from children who aren't your own—you are not responsible for them. But another difference is that your child's behavior reflects on you, and when he misbehaves you feel like a failure—in addition to feeling frustrated and angry. Also, according to some authorities, parents feel that they have every right to hit their children because they are *their* children—they are possessions, or extensions of the parents.

When you are really furious, try taking a step backward and pretending that your child is not your child. Think of him or her as the son or daughter of a friend or neighbor. It may take a little practice, but it can be done and it helps. (And it is a good habit to get into whether or not you are angry, for although we may be responsible for our children until they are grown, we don't *own* them—they are separate people, and all too often we forget that.)

Whether we hit or not, however, the anger we feel must be dealt with. And that begins with a firm resolve to pay attention to anger as it occurs. Don't tell yourself you shouldn't feel that way—it is pointless because you feel as you feel and no command or injunction can change that.

Having once recognized anger and, hopefully, not judged yourself for feeling it, let off steam. Talk to someone. *Especially* if you are married, talk to your husband—you need his support and he should know what's going on in his family. If that's not enough, call a hotline and rant and rave anonymously. Or, call a friend. Talking really does help. I have several friends who serve as my sounding boards, and I've been known to provide the same function for other people. Two women I know have an agreement with each other—they can call at any time and really let loose. Someone in similar circumstances, whose feelings are much like your own, is an ideal candidate.

If you absolutely must hit to vent your rage, then hit something other than a child. Remember the pillow and the encounterbats? When you feel like hitting, go into your bedroom, snatch a pillow off your bed, turn it into your target, and give it a name. Hit it and call it by its name, and every other name in the book and do it until your anger is spent.

In all probability, however, most of us will never arrive at the child- or pillow-punching stage if we consistently deal verbally with our anger as it occurs. Nor, with the exception of the parent who was abused as a child, would we worry about one spank leading to full-scale violence, or about the myth that emotional abuse is just as serious as physical abuse.

I'm firmly convinced that many reasonably stable, conscientious, and intelligent parents have got the idea that virtually *anything* they feel, do, or say will result in some sort of child abuse, such as screaming on one occasion, "You are driving me crazy!", thereby marking a child for life. Given the way in which the term "emotional abuse" is bandied about, there isn't a parent alive who has not been guilty of it—or experienced it personally during childhood.

But emotional abuse is far more complicated than many parents might think. It consists of *habitually* insulting and demeaning a child, neglecting him or her, withholding affection, and *really* scaring a child—for example, frequently threatening him or her with abandonment. It is generally a *combination* of more than one of these behaviors, and often also includes physical abuse. In light of that, I do not see an occasional healthy outburst of anger, even if the words used in the delivery are insulting, as emotional abuse.

So, tell your child that you're so mad you can't see straight. Don't worry about whether you are using all the proper jargon or sending conflicting messages—once you've come to terms with your anger you can concern yourself with the fine art of communication.

But whatever you do, remember not to make the mistake of asking a child why he did something—why he hurled a dish across the room or even set the cat on fire. Remember that children often don't know *why* and you will just further aggravate yourself when you press for an answer.

If verbalizing your feelings is too risky at a given time, there are other ways you can express anger and let your children know when you've had enough. For example, one woman told me that when she feels as if she's reaching the edge of the ledge, she dons a baseball hat. She explained that her children, three and five years old, understand that when the hat goes on, she's boiling mad. "It works," she says. "When I put the hat on, they behave like angels. And when I get good results, my anger starts to fade."

Another woman sits at the kitchen table and quietly rolls up a newspaper, threateningly turning it into a weapon (that wouldn't hurt a fly) and she maintains that her children pick up the signal that they are really going to get it and then they simmer down.

Still another counts. Why do we forget, when our kids are driving us crazy and we can't seem to control either them or our anger, that counting works to do both?

When my children watch television together they fight. I can't stand it. I used to yell at them and threaten and get so angry that I wanted to tear them apart. One day someone said, "Turn off the TV set." So obvious. I turned off the set and the children stopped fighting and got the message that I was angry. And, of course, since they didn't want me to intermittently turn off the set, they didn't return to doing battle with one another.

The "Processing" Solution

Something I've learned to do with anger is to "process it out." When I feel that initial flash of anger that is disproportionate to the situation, I stick to my firm resolve not to act physically on that feeling. I then allow myself to feel white-hot rage course through my body—from the top of my head down to my toes. And while I'm doing so, I allow myself to be righteously indignant and, in the privacy of my own mind, think the darkest and angriest of all thoughts. In a matter of minutes I can feel the intensity of the anger begin to ebb and can figure out just what it was that made me so mad. One day, for example, I was trying to work and the day was getting shorter all too quickly. It was summer and the kids were home, making noise and getting underfoot. I was in the middle of a complicated thought when Lisa, then seven, burst into the room, tracking dirt as she came, and said, "I thought we were going to go to the store." Her tone was accusing. I became infuriated. Logically I was infuriated at the interruption on top of the confusion of the day. I felt like slapping my daughter. I sat like a stone, feeling my anger, and as it started to move out of my body, I realized that I wasn't angry at Lisa at all. I wasn't even angry at the tone she used or the interruption. I was mad because I didn't want to go to the store—I absolutely detest any sort of shopping—and she reminded me that I had to.

Processing works just as well when the cause of anger is actually justified by the behavior of the child. It does take practice and it depends on one's ability to acknowledge anger as it occurs and not feel guilty about it. I recommend using other ways of venting your emotions along with it when you first try it.

My Grandmother's Solutions (They Work!)

My grandmother had two stock suggestions for working through anger and frustration and neither one of them called for the denial of emotions: write it out, work it off. They as old as time, and I sometimes think we forget how effective these devices are.

Writing it out works wonders for me. Every unsayable insult you can possibly think of can go down on that sheet of paper. You can say things you wouldn't even say to a psychiatrist. And if you hang onto the pages and read them later, you can gain many insights that will help you to put your feelings into perspective. Some people write letters to the people who anger them and then don't send them. Others just scratch out their feelings on loose scraps of paper. Still others maintain carefully kept journals. One woman who keeps a journal is the mother of eight children who take turns driving her crazy, and frequently do so in concert. When I mentioned to her once that she seemed to cope so well, she said, "You should see my journal. Not a day goes by that I don't make entries. On second thought, nobody should see it. It is filled with the ravings of a lunatic."

You can work off your anger by going into the yard and furiously pulling weeds, shoveling snow, sweeping walks, or you can stay inside and scrub walls, clean out closets, vigorously vacuum carpets. I have found that it helps even more to think actively about your anger while you are working, and hold imaginary conversations with the object of your wrath. One of the fringe benefits of using the energy of your anger constructively is that you accomplish something and feel better about yourself as a result.

And another good way to use that energy is to try to change your situation. Let's say you are a working mother, trapped in the house all weekend with two children under the age of three; the oldest has been clinging to your skirts and whining half the day and spending the other half flinging himself on the floor and getting into mischief. The baby has been fussy most of the day. You could rummage through Dr. Spock or Dr. Salk to find out why your three-year-old is acting this way and learn that it's because he needs more attention than you are giving him. You might find out that the baby is crying for the same reason. You might then conclude that somehow you have got to give both of them some loving attention *simultaneously*. Only you don't want to, and you don't know how to give undivided attention to two children at the same time. Lurking in the back of your mind, in any case, is the sense that if you are going to do any touching it will be hitting.

At this point, if you can control your temper, you can either begrudgingly give the children the attention you are led to believe they need and run the risk that the rivalry they feel toward one another will result in demands for even more attention, or you can withhold your attention and feel guilty. Or, you can say, in the middle of your anger, "Goddamn it, I'm a human being and I don't have to take this crap anymore." You pick up the three-year-old and put him in his room and tell him *firmly* that he has to stay there and play with his toys until you tell him he can come out; you close the door to the baby's room. Then you go to the phone and call a sitter service or a sitter you know, and make arrangements to get away as soon as possible for a few hours. It may turn out that you can't do so as soon as you'd like (*right this minute*), but it will give you some time to look forward to—something to cling to and something to validate your sense that you are a person, too.

With the children in their rooms, you may then want to sit down, pencil and pad in hand, and think of any other specific realistic ways you can improve your situation. The older child, for example, routinely gets into the linen closet and tosses out the towels you've just folded and put away, or both get into mischief in other parts of the house. Okay, this is the day that you flip to Chapter Nine to find out how to childproof your house to protect both the house and your sanity and make plans to do it. If you have the items you need on hand, do it. If not, plan to pick them up the next time you are out.

Or, if you are a housewife, you can work out, in your mind and on paper, the logistics of returning to your old job or finding a new one and arranging for someone else to look after the children. Even if you don't want to return to work at this particular time, this can be an illuminating and therapeutic exercise. You may discover, for example, in the process, that a part-time job just might be the answer for you. And just thinking about doing something besides being a mother reinforces you as a person and helps to get rid of some of the resentment you might feel over being diminished.

I have no definitive answer for every parent, but I can share my own sense of hard-won perspective. As regards spanking in particular, I see it as appropriate only when it is part of a parent's overall approach to discipline and includes love, fair play, the making and enforcement of reasonable rules, and the healthy expression of one's own feelings—and never as a tension reliever for parents carrying around bottled-up rage.

To do no harm either to yourself or your child begins with the acceptance of anger as a normal human emotion. When one learns to recognize not only anger as normal, but also the need some parents feel to get even with a child for wreaking havoc in their lives, then the tendency to store it away in Dr. Rubin's "slush fund," as well as the need for revenge, does diminish. And eventually, when we've caught up on the backlog of anger, Rubin tells us the simple acknowledgment of it as it occurs can become a form of tension-relieving expression.

6

Creating Your Own
Lifelines

An extreme example of a mother who put the energy of her anger to work to change her situation is Jolly K. Jolly was *completely* without a support system—a lifeline. The only coping device she had for her anger and frustration was beating her child. She didn't want to beat her child. She didn't want to reinforce her sense that she was worthless. So she spent three years trying to get help for herself and the child she was abusing. Finally, when she became so enraged that she threw a tantrum in the office of a social worker, she was assigned to a therapist. During one stormy session with him, she railed against the system, saying that there should be a program to help mothers who had problems like hers. Her therapist said simply, "Why don't you do something about it?" She did. Along with another woman, she founded Mothers Anonymous and served as the driving force that turned it into a nationwide organization. And all because she needed a lifeline—someone to reach out to when she reached the brink of despair.

The success of Jolly's organization, later renamed Parents Anonymous, has stimulated the development of similar organizations, all of which stand ready to reach out to parents and offer support, no matter what their circumstances might be. There are well over 500 groups (operating under various names—Parental Stress Hotline, CALM, COPE, TALK, CARING) and they have sprung up all over the United States. Most of them are open twenty-four hours a day, seven days a week, and most offer a range of services including respite child care, home visits, and parent discussion groups. Carefully screened and trained, the volunteers who staff the hotlines offer support, understanding, and friendship to mothers who have reached the ends of their ropes and feel they have nowhere else to turn. Empathetic and nonjudgmental, hotline volunteers often have experienced many of the same feelings the callers express. They know how to listen, when to ask a question and when not to, and are sensitive to the clues that may indicate a need for more help than can be given over the telephone.

The most important thing that the volunteers who operate these services do is to let mothers know that they aren't alone when they feel so isolated with their problems and negative feelings. Any woman who is overwhelmed by her feelings can call and need not give her name, so she can talk as openly as she wishes. When more help is needed, the volunteers can either point parents in the right direction or make arrangements for them to receive the services they need—from child care to counseling—because these organizations maintain current and carefully checked referral files on all parent/child services in the community.

I've had dozens of mothers tell me that once they have located a hotline and noted the number, just having the number handy and knowing they had a place to turn was enough to get them through their toughest days. As one mother put it, "Knowing I can call if I need to really does help—so much that I don't have to call. Keeping that number in my wallet is my security blanket."

When Jolly created her lifeline, she started the ball rolling to create one important lifeline for all mothers, which in turn has started the ball rolling for other lifelines that can keep mothers from going crazy. Much of the time, however, because the resources of these groups are sparse, mothers must create most of the other lifelines they will need.

The Need for Solitude

A mother of four preschoolers told me that she was once so desperate that she went into the bedroom and locked the door, went into the adjoining bathroom and locked that door, and then sat down in the shower—"just to be alone." She was so driven by her need for solitude at that moment that she couldn't even worry about leaving her toddler unsupervised with free run of the house.

And the mother of two relatively civilized school-aged children explained how she felt one summer day when the children had been home with her for several weeks: "Even when the day is a relatively quiet one, the accumulation of all of the others that went before gets to you. It is just the constant presence of others—especially if those others are children—that I can't stand. Today, I can't even tolerate having a child—no matter who he belongs to—in the house." She explained that the sound of her son clipping items out of his magazines was like Chinese water torture: "Snip, snip, snip, breathe, breathe, breathe, until I think I'll go mad."

Ah yes, the summer. At just about the same time that I thought I wouldn't survive it one year, a friend of mine *quite literally* feared she wouldn't make it when she woke up one morning spitting up blood. "This is it," she told herself. "They say stress will do it to you—now I've probably got throat cancer or TB." Well, now, we know that everyone worries incessantly about cancer—if we move the wrong way, we'll get it is the message we receive. So, this woman called an eye, ear, nose, and throat specialist and told his receptionist that she needed to see the doctor *immediately*. After the examination the doctor told her, "Really, Mrs. Phillips, there's nothing seriously wrong— you've just broken some capillaries in your throat." How, my friend wanted to know, does someone do that? "From straining the vocal cords, Mrs. Phillips. From too much yelling."

"What were you yelling?" I asked.

"Among other things," she said, "GO OUTSIDE—LEAVE ME ALONE! Naturally, I felt guiltier about that than yelling at them when they were doing things they weren't supposed to do."

Most people need to have time to themselves—time away from any other people—just to collect their wits and recharge their batteries. But not only are most young mothers who choose to stay home deprived of this basic need for personal space, they are subject, on an open-ended basis, to small people who need care, make noise, make messes, get into mischief, and cling to their mothers. And even those of us who work find ourselves sharing these problems some of the time.

The Need for Helpers and How to Find Them

Many of us do not have easy access to child care. We do not have a reservoir of grandparents and aunties and uncles to take over for us. For some, the expense of paying a sitter during the hours we can be there seems unjustifiable and unaffordable; for others it actually *is* unaffordable. But mostly I think that guilt is the deciding factor in whether or not a mother makes arrangements to have time for herself. First of all, a mother may feel guilty just for wanting to be away from her children because she is laboring under a sense that it is not socially acceptable for a mother to feel that way—that there is something wrong with her for having such "abnormal" desires. I cannot believe that there exists any human adult who relishes being with young children on a continuing basis. I think closer to the truth are the words of a psychiatrist Helen DeRosis, co-author of *The Book of Hope,* who says, "Some parents are just plain bored by long periods of their children's company. They don't mind taking care of their children's concrete needs, taking them places, but just to be with a little child for a long period of time is something that drives some parents up the wall. I consider a long period to be anywhere from one hour up."

And it is a fact that most mothers spend far more than one hour a day, whether it is companionable time or not, listening to a child talk and answering his or her questions while taking care of the child's needs. It is hardly abnormal to wish to spend at least a little time doing otherwise.

Another reservation that parents I have talked to seem to have about leaving their children when there are no family members to take over is that they are abandoning their children to the care of strangers—who might neglect them. In the first place, if you hire reliable sitters through an agency you know or on the recommendation of other parents, the chance of neglect is rather remote. A sitter who has not been constantly with your child or children quite likely will have *more* patience than you have.

A very wise pediatrician told me that children need to be away from their parents just as much as parents need to be away from their children. Warning of the dangers inherent in constant contact, he said, "Sometimes young children become whiny and cantankerous because *they* are tired of being with *you.* They need relief from your parenting of them. He also pointed out that the child who does not become accustomed to being left in the care of others is likely to feel *truly* abandoned when he or she is left with someone else when there is no choice in the matter. "It is impossible to say with certainty," he said, "that you will always be able to care for your child yourself. What if you have to go to the hospital? Return to work? Go on a trip and cannot take your child with you? If he hasn't gotten used to your being periodically away he's more likely to think you are never coming back. Furthermore, the child who has only been looked after by his parents has a harder time making adjustments when he goes off to school." Therefore, if you are a working mother plagued by guilt, remember those words—the chances are you are doing your child a favor by not being with him or her all of the time, in that you are imbuing him or her with a sense of independence.

For those who might suggest that reliable sitters are hard to find, I must counter by saying that I never had any such difficulties. And with the exception of those mothers who work outside the home and need full-time child care (which is sometimes hard to come by without really looking for it), most mothers who make an effort to find good child care say the same thing.

Finally, there's the expense. Mothers seem to view the fees they pay a sitter as some sort of luxury—an unnecessary expense. That is partly because it is an obvious one that families "can do without." But mostly, I think, it is because, unless it is a material item that a woman might "need," there is some reluctance on her part to spend money on herself. Husbands often don't understand that getting away is absolutely essential—unless it's to get away with them—so they only tend to reinforce the strange mix of feelings that many mothers have about arranging for child care.

Of course, many fathers don't understand simply because they aren't on constant child-care duty. Lacking understanding for what it might be like to be with children all the time can work for you: if he doesn't think it's so bad, then let him take care of the kids on a Saturday. Perhaps he'll gain empathy and offer to spell you more often, or perhaps he'll do as one father did and tell you to hire a sitter to come in regularly so he doesn't have to do it. Yes, yes, I know that the reason for turning it over to father regularly is so that he can spend more time with the children and they all can develop enriching relationships with one another. However, I'm a realist, and I think many fathers would just as soon cop out; it is easier for them to do because they don't have any guilt about not liking to be with their children for long periods of time simply because it is okay for fathers to feel that way and express that view. So, take it any way you can get it. Who knows? Maybe he'll love it so much he'll switch roles if you're a housewife.

But you need more than father sitting on a Saturday every once in a while. And the fact is, child care isn't that expensive. Because I felt more comfortable leaving our children with mature sitters I have always paid premium sitting fees. The agency I used when Lisa and Adam still required sitters currently charges four dollars per hour for a minimum of four hours. While this may seem to be steep, little else will give you the peace of mind that $16.00 worth of time away will. When you consider that counseling currently runs at least $75.00 an hour, and the best advice a sensitive therapist might give to an overwhelmed mother is, "You need time off," $16.00 is a bargain. Another way of looking at it is to ask what else that amount of money can buy. At a good sale at Macy's, it can't even buy a new blouse. And a new blouse can't do for you what a few hours of respite can do. If you absolutely cannot afford to use an agency, you can place an advertisement on the bulletin board of your local high school—there are many teenagers who would be thrilled to sit for less.

Another possibility for children three years of age or older is preschool. From the standpoint of how positive it is for children, I heartily recommend it whenever it is financially feasible. The stay-at-home mother is given relief, while at the same time, her children are enriched. I cannot say enough for the value of preschool to young children.

Whether you work or not, you may be into a pattern of taking your children shopping with you, but here is what one wise mother had to say on that subject: "When my children were very young, even though I worked all week and was away from them, I hired sitters while I did my marketing and ran my errands on Saturday. I am convinced that I spent less money at the grocery store than I would have had I taken the children with me, simply because I could concentrate on what I was doing." And recently I was told by a friend who works for a large chain that store owners and managers prefer mothers to other shoppers because women with children along always spend more money than lone, thoughtful shoppers. (Perhaps this is why plans for a child-care center at one of our local shopping centers were scrapped without any explanation.) Aside from the economics, I would advise mothers to avoid running errands with their children just on the strength of the fact that coping with preschoolers, and even older children, in public places such as supermarkets or banks often leads to incredible tensions and, as we all know, embarrassing and damaging explosions.

If you cannot afford regular sitting fees, or do not have friends or relatives who will sit with your children, consider joining a baby-sitting cooperative or helping to get one started. Inherent advantages are that the sitting is frequently done in the home of the one doing it, so not only do you get a rest for a while, but so does your house.

If you can afford child care, if you can find sitters who will sit with your children in *their* homes, it is absolutely wonderful to be alone in your own house—to once in a while have the children off somewhere, in good hands, when you don't have any place in particular to go but would just like to do some of your chores or pursue some interest in peace without interruption.

Your Own Space

I feel very strongly about uninterrupted time, for I have long felt something I couldn't quite put my finger on, much less define as serious. It seemed petty—an immature way to feel—but when my children were very young and home all the time, even when things were going smoothly, I sometimes felt madness setting in. I sometimes still do when they are home a lot (for example, during the summer) and restless. It isn't just that the frequent random interruptions (especially prevalent when children are young) are annoying and interfere with what a mother may be doing, but I think they have the same net effect on people as not allowing them to dream. I jokingly used to call this the "thought interruptus syndrome." When I now think about it, I can define it as serious. Researchers have found that when people are not allowed to dream, for instance, schizophrenia can result. What about when people are not allowed to have free-flowing thoughts, or even concentrated ones, without constant interruptions? I think this can produce a madness outside of the general confusion, frustration, and guilt that are part of being a mother, and I therefore feel that it's vital that mothers have the space just to *be*—just to think, let the thoughts flow, in order to maintain emotional well-being.

I cannot point to any research on what happens when people are suffering the "thought interruptus syndrome," but perhaps one day when mothers are considered important persons, some investigators might look into it and discover this up-to-now invisible madness-making element in the motherhood role.

Meanwhile, I cannot emphasize enough that relief from parenting and having personal space are vital to a mother's well-being. And a mother's well-being, we are told, is vital to that of her children. This need, or mutual need, is nothing to feel ashamed of. It has existed from the day mothers were invented, and in fact, in the not too distant past, respite from child care was fairly routine and accepted—when it was also fairly routine for more than one generation to live under the same roof. In any case, you would not put off getting a tooth filled or seeing a doctor when you need to, and I put getting away from your children on the same level.

It was after my first book was published that I received a letter from a well-known pediatrician. He wrote, "If mothers could just get away from mothering without feeling ashamed for needing to, so many of the problems they have could be prevented."

And one woman who had chosen to stay home all day with her children instead of returning to her old job took this advice and said to me, "You can't schedule your bad days and plan to be away when you have them, but knowing I'm going to be out of the house for part of one day each week or that a sitter will take the kids home really helps to keep me from falling apart during those terrible times that we all have—I live from Thursday to Thursday and it makes the days in between much easier to handle."

Some mothers, in addition to simply needing some periodic solitude, need other outlets for fulfillment—to pursue interests that are difficult to pursue around young children. But whether it is to gain time to be alone or to do something else besides mothering, periodic relief from the constant responsibility and company of children is an *absolute and basic necessity*. It is not good for the creative person to defer the near compulsion to write or paint until some day in the future when the children are in school. Nor is it good for someone who wants to play tennis or who loves to read to set aside these symbols of her personhood. The frustration that can build up without these outlets isn't healthy for either the parents or the children.

Solitude Is Not the Same as Isolation

While we all need solitude—time just for ourselves—the one thing that mothers do not need is *isolation*. Especially isolation from other adults—and more especially, isolation from other adults while in the company of one or more small children.

But isolation, as noted previously, is built into the motherhood role. In contrast to the way in which our foremothers functioned—doing some of their chores together, relying on each other instead of television to provide day-time entertainment as they folded the clothes, and supported by a tradition that found more than one generation living in a family home— today's mothers, even working mothers, do most of their work at home in solitude. Instead of chatting with each other as they peel potatoes, exchanging bits of folk wisdom or talking openly about motherhood being a bit of a cross to bear, they listen to the hum of their appliances, the whine of their children, and the din of their TV sets while trying out all the new products that promise to make their home cleaner than any in history.

What cuts mothers off from other adults? Sometimes it is the goal of trying to maintain a perfectly kept house, which doesn't allow time for visiting with friends, that isolates a mother; sometimes it is a recent move that has left a mother without friends. And then some mothers who become depressed purposely cut themselves off. But whatever the reason, the results can be disastrous. This sort of isolation, according to psychologist Philip G. Zimbardo of Stanford University, is conducive to madness even in the stablest of individuals. Zimbardo claims that when a person has an experience that deeply affects his or her mental peace, they need to know that others have had similar experiences in order to reassure them that they aren't going insane. He cites isolation from other adults as the primary factor in a person not being able to check the validity of his or her own experiences: "Under such circumstances," says Zimbardo, "beliefs are readily transformed into delusions." It is not difficult to see how a mother who is struggling with the paradoxes and conflicts of parenthood, isolated from other adults, might suspect that her negative feelings are symptoms of psychosis.

I would say that the one single thing that can make a difference between a mother hanging in there during those difficult years with young children and flipping out is whether she has positive contact with other adults. A support system that would provide this might include an understanding husband, a helpful mother or other relatives, work, or some combination.

Good Friends Can Be Your Answer

While I would very much like to take full credit for turning my own negative cycle into a positive one, I can't. Right up there with having the sense to see child care as a necessity and doing something about it on a regular basis, is the fact that I had (and continue to have) very good friends. When I started falling apart, after I had stopped working and was home alone with my children, I was very ashamed of myself for not being able to manage my life and my emotions better, and I really didn't want to see other people. Nor did I want them to see me—I didn't want my friends to see me in such a state—I still had *some* pride, after all. But damn, they wouldn't leave me alone. It really irritated me that they would construct all kinds of Mickey Mouse excuses to call me up and bother me—jar me out of the depression and self-flagellation I was indulgently wallowing in—or they'd "just happen to be in the neighborhood," and drop in.

But when I look back to that time, I know I can never adequately express the gratitude I've since come to feel. I am a lucky woman indeed. As much as I needed to, I would not have reached out to my friends at that time. But I didn't have to. Their support system was there—completely built in, over my objections to its very existence. And it did not allow me to be "locked in a cage" alone with young children for interminable stretches—at a time in my life when that would have been the most disastrous.

Although eventually my friends and I got around to talking about what was bothering me, ostensibly this was not what was behind all the attention I was receiving. I recall one day when a woman friend came by, plopped down, and asked me if there was any coffee made. I wanted her to leave ("This is not a goddamn restaurant") but was too timid to say so. She couldn't have come at a worse time. I was especially upset that day because on top of everything else my son had done something that I perceived to be as serious as a bank job. For some reason, I started babbling about it. Then I was crying. And *then,* I noticed with a shock that my friend was laughing. She took my hand and said, "I'm not laughing at you—I really can feel your pain. But you know, this whole situation with Adam is hilarious." And it was. And I started laughing. And then we started swapping stories of all the things kids do that are perfectly terrible at the time but very funny in retrospect. And, of course, how really funny our own reactions can be. I couldn't remember when I'd felt better—both physically and emotionally. You know, sometimes laughter really *is* the best medicine.

Similar times with other friends, often more than one at a time, continued, and the discussions about how painful motherhood really could be were open and free. We all—those of us who were parents—learned that we were in the same boat and that some of us had more trouble handling our feelings than others.

I didn't know it at the time, but my friends were a large part of my lifeline. They wouldn't let me resign from the human race; they let me know they were there if I needed them (without insulting me by suggesting that I was in such bad shape that I did need them). Finally, and perhaps most importantly, they didn't allow me to suffer that indescribable loneliness that comes from being imprisoned behind four walls of a house, with the only companions your young children and continual negative noise in the head.

The isolation mothers experience has many faces. There is the actual physical isolation that all by itself can be lonely as hell; there is the loneliness that comes from being bored with the work and the conversations that one has with people who, because of their ages, have rather limited interests—cookies, fighting with each other, toys, mess, and mischief. But when it is combined with the isolation that Zimbardo speaks of—the sense of being so very alone in your feelings, and perhaps fearful that you are actually going mad, it can be unbearable.

I experienced only a small measure of it, thanks to my friends. But it was enough. Enough to make me want to shout at young, troubled, isolated mothers, "Don't do this to yourselves! Don't lock yourself up with your children by denying yourself time away from them, and then when it gets to you, cut yourself off from other adults!" I want to say, "I know just how you feel. I know you don't want to see anyone. I know you fear you will be judged and that you are frightened. But *see people!* See your friends, make friends if you don't have any. The regular company of other adults is vital to your mental health!"

And I know it is especially difficult if you are new to a community, but there are organizations and groups that can help. Most branches of the YWCA offer seminars and meetings—some are just of general interest, but some reach out to mothers, allowing them to meet other women in similar circumstances. And most communities have Newcomers, Nomads, or Welcome Wagon Clubs. My recommendation of these groups is not an idle one—I have met with their members and my impressions are that they are composed of friendly, giving, interesting people—most of whom are in one of the same situations you may be in. A fringe benefit is that often these organizations have baby-sitting co-ops.

One young mother, new in the community and alone except for a new baby and a husband who went off to the office each day, told me, "Newcomers quite literally saved my life. I didn't know anyone. I was trapped in the house with a screaming infant and when I received an invitation to a luncheon and went, I made friends. I'm involved in the baby-sitting co-op, and that alone has opened up my life in many ways I hadn't thought possible during my darkest days."

The Need for a Support System and How to Build One

After my first book was published, I appeared on a television talk show with three other women, one of whom was the well-known psychologist Eda LeShan. One of the other women on the show, an established author and the mother of three children, said, at one point, "I just don't understand all this. When I'd rather do something besides be with my children or start to feel a little crazy, I just call my mother and tell her I'm coming to leave the kids, or I just drop them off on her doorstep. Also when I don't know what to do about something, I call my mother, or if she's not available, I call my friends and keep calling until I find one who can offer a suggestion."

I will always love Eda LeShan for jumping in before I had to respond defensively, and pointing out that this woman had a rather unique and superb support system. She said something to the effect, "*You* have a mother you *can* leave your children with any time, and one you can talk with. You also feel secure enough to call your many friends. You are *lucky!* Most mothers do not have these resources."

Indeed. Most of us do not have built-in ideal situations. Thus, after determining what they might be, we must create them. The good news is that most of us can do so. We can hire people to take care of our children, we can choose not to be lonely—we can create our own lifelines. One woman, who did this only after the situation with her family developed into a full-scale crisis, told me, "I never knew before of all the wonderful services that are available to mothers—I never knew that there really are so many nice people in the world until I needed help. Had I been aware, I could have avoided so much needless suffering."

Now, let us review the resources available, and how you can establish lifelines for yourself.

- My heartfelt advice to anyone in need of support is: *Get training*. Knowing what can go wrong *before* you've reached the end of your rope is your best protection against unrealistic expectations of yourself as a parent and of your child. Parenting and coping skills *can* be learned. In many communities courses now exist designed to teach parents how to deal with stressful parenting situations and any negative feelings they may be having towards their children. Courses are often available for parents of children who are between birth and preschool age. To find out if any classes exist in your area, call you local hospital, your obstetrician, Adult Education, a parental stress hotline (see telephone numbers below), the YWCA, or your local Natural Childbirth Association.

- You need somewhere to turn *when* you've reached the end of your rope. Sympathetic friends, of course, are ideal, but not all of us feel comfortable about talking to them about our darkest feelings. Find out what *parent*-centered services exist in your community. To do this, check the classified section of your newspaper, the Yellow Pages, call your local hospital, or contact the YWCA or your Family Services Association. Ask about Parental Stress Hotline Services or Parents Anonymous hotlines and groups. You can call Parents Anonymous toll-free in California at 1-800-352-0386; from elsewhere in the nation, the number is 1-800-421-0353 to find out if there's a group in your area. (In some areas you may not need to dial "1" first.) If there are no parent lines, using the same resources, find out if there is a Suicide and Crisis Hotline, CONNECT, or CARE (the volunteers on these lines are similarly screened and trained). When you find a number to call, record it and keep it handy. Do this *before* you have a crisis, if possible.

- And then, if you ever need to let off steam but feel you have nowhere to turn, use that number and freely pour out your heart. You are completely anonymous when you call, and even if you decide to give your name, the records of these organizations are held in the strictest of confidence. You can tell them absolutely anything. (And you can use the line even if you aren't going bonkers, to find out what other services exist.)

- Accept that you are a normal human being and not a super-woman or a paragon of patience, and therefore you absolutely must, if you are a homemaker, have regular relief from that job, or if you are a working mother, relief from *both* of your jobs. You must have some child-care resources. Here are some suggestions.

1. If you are lucky, family members can take over, so take advantage of any offers to do so that are extended. Also, *ask* for help.

2. Contact a baby-sitting agency and use a variety of sitters so that several will become familiar with your children and be available to you. Ask your friends and acquaintances for the names of reliable sitters; use them and keep them on tap. Don't rely on just one sitter—it is better to have about six you can call on.

3. Join a baby-sitting co-op; look for one through hotline groups and local chapters of Family Services Association, YWCA, Nomads, Newcomers, Welcome Wagon, or the Natural Child-birth Association; also co-ops can be found through some churches and nursery school mothers' groups.

4. Get together with several friends and neighbors and start your own co-op.

- What do you like to do? Play tennis, take classes, paint? You *need* this outlet, so, after you make your child-care arrangements, do at least one thing that is yours alone.

- Combat maternal isolation. If you are new to the area and do not have friends, don't stay in that rut. So you have all the boxes still to unpack, but after you've unpacked the *essentials,* find out about those clubs that are available to newcomers to an area. You need friends more than you need perfect order.

  If you aren't new to the area but tend to isolate yourself,

don't do it. If you feel you don't have any friends, then meet people through some of the community organizations. Get to know your neighbors, which is always a good idea in any case because you often can rely on them to help in an emergency.

When you establish good friendships with other mothers, you may come to realize that all of us—the human among us, that is—have problems and negative feelings about being parents. At some point, you and your friends will be able to honestly share your feelings and hence lighten your burdens. This is something I have learned through experience—that honesty begets honesty, and it does help.

- Don't forget your pediatrician. If you have a regular pediatrician, he or she can give you more support, advice, and help than you might realize. If you have a problem, *call.* If you can't because you don't feel comfortable with the doctor you have chosen, find one you *can* talk easily with. Our pediatrician once told me, after I said something about not wanting to bother him over things that might not be important: "You call, and you let me worry about whether it's important or not—never let that keep you from calling."

- Get training. In many communities today, there are parenting classes that go beyond teaching you how to feed and bathe the baby, classes that focus on what parents can expect at various stages of development. These meetings can provide parents with a built-in support group. To find out what's available in your area, call your local hospitals or community college systems.

7

The Complete Guide to Maternal Guilt

If you have but one life to live, live it with high self-esteem! It is your choice, a decision not made in the heavens but in your head. It is YOUR General Accounting System that posts the report that your self-esteem is high or low . . . you have probably tagged the low self-esteem label on yourself . . . Low has got to go! Think positively of yourself, set meaningful goals that require some measure of ambition, industry, and perseverance to attain. Then, learn to evaluate your accomplishments in an honest and realistic fashion.

> Philip G. Zimbardo
> SHYNESS, WHAT IT IS, WHAT TO DO ABOUT IT

If what you're doing is making you sick, stop doing it.

> Abraham H. Maslow
> RELIGIONS, VALUES, AND PEAK-EXPERIENCES

One woman told me that the first step she took to get her self-respect back was to treat her child better. "I hated the way I treated him, resented him for making me feel guilty, hated myself. And one day I said to myself, 'NO MORE!' Since I started treating my child better, I don't feel guilty all the time, thus really feel better about him, and hence have less reason to mistreat him."

The "looking out for number one" approach to life may work well when it comes to (temporarily) shedding guilt feelings for grossly selfish and inconsiderate behavior. But it won't do much for your ability to develop friendships with others, and I don't think, over the long haul, it will do much for your relationship with yourself. Thus, I guess I would have to say that it takes much more to really do something for a drooping self-esteem than simply to "look out for number one," or *"feel* better about yourself to do better." Like the woman who changed the way she acted toward her son, you've got to *do* better to feel better—switch it around.

The most important thing you will *do,* then, to work toward having feelings that you're a worthwhile person—to turn a negative cycle into a positive one—will be making the decision to do so. The next important step will be to set goals—writing them down—for self-improvement, and the most important thing you will do while setting those goals will be to make sure they are realistic. If, for example, you decide that you will feel better about yourself if you lose weight, don't set as your goal losing twenty-five pounds the first month. Or, more to the point, if you have trouble maintaining your composure in the company of young children, don't set as your goal being totally serene and understanding and fully in control of the environment while the children drive you to distraction. Instead, set as a goal developing a little more patience. And if you hate being around young children, don't demand of yourself that in four days you will do a total about-face. In other words, don't set yourself up for failure by setting as your goal *perfection* of feelings and performance. Do not replace your present program for failure— the glossy motherhood image—with a slightly different one that produces the same sense of failure.

How to Reduce Your Storehouse of Guilt

The building of self-esteem requires that you get rid of most of your guilts and *do whatever you can to avoid situations that will create new ones.* I say "most" with good reason, for guilt in and of itself is not a totally bad thing—it has a function in making you accountable to yourself. But when the guilt causes you to lose your sense of self-worth to such an extent that you are caught in a trap of guiltily proving, time and time again, what a rotten person you are, then it ceases to have this very useful function. And mothers, because of the job they have been handed, are especially vulnerable to that crippling sort of guilt that feeds upon itself.

The range of things about which a mother can feel guilty is vast. Mothers look for and collect guilt the way philatelists collect stamps. They build storehouses of it that perpetually (and more effectively as they grow) serve to reinforce feelings of utter inadequacy. And when their storehouses become full enough, they have trouble functioning, and then they feel guilty about *that.*

By the time my children were five and six years old, I had accumulated a list of things I should do or should have done for them (it was retroactive to Day One) and didn't because I didn't want to or didn't have the time; the list was so long it was overwhelming. Not only did I not play games with them often, I didn't do kitchen crafts, didn't get them started with a vegetable garden, didn't get involved in co-op nursery school (because I just *knew* I couldn't take it), didn't put them in little strollers and proudly parade them down the street, didn't read stories to them every day, didn't teach them to read when they were three years old (everyone else did—it was the thing to do), didn't join them when they finger-painted, didn't take them to the zoo very often, didn't make toys for them, didn't take them camping. And—oh yes, I almost forgot—I never made my own baby food!

This is only a partial list, of course, and when I stacked even that up against what I did for them—took good care of them, cuddled them and genuinely loved them, it didn't look very good. It especially didn't look very good when I added to my list the fact that I didn't always like being a mother. But in a rare moment of self-love, it came to me that my not doing all that was required of the typical middle-class suburban mother had not appreciably scarred my children for life. So I forgave myself.

I must admit, however, that I had some help in that act of mercy. A very dear friend shared with me an exercise for self-forgiveness that I will now pass along to you. She told me that she became so tired of carrying around the burden of self-hatred that she decided to forgive herself for all past wrongdoings against all people, and then forgive herself for all of her inadequacies, bad thoughts, and impure feelings. One day when she was totally alone in her house, she took the phone off the hook and pulled the drapes. She would be, she said, "not at home" during this period if anyone should drop by. She then went into the bedroom, sat down on the bed, and started consciously to recall as many things as possible over which she had suffered (and was suffering) punishing guilt. She went way back to a time when she was not a mother but just a small child herself. "The large guilts and the small ones marched across my mind. Some were unbearable, some were embarrassing, some were absurd. I wanted to push the serious ones back down where they'd been safely stored, but I didn't. I looked at them all. One at a time. Sometimes they would crowd in on me, but I made each wait its turn. I relived each incident—each sin. Sometimes my face would burn with shame, sometimes I would sob. I reminded myself that to forgive is divine, even if it is you you are forgiving. Then I said, 'I forgive you,' in every way I could think of, using different words so that I wouldn't allow myself any 'outs.' I did this with each and every one of my guilty sins until I felt truly forgiven.

"This was not unlike baring your soul to a very good friend who would not stand in judgment of you, or going to confession and receiving absolution for your sins. But there was one very important difference. *No matter who forgives you,* or how *completely* they do, no matter who understands and tells you that you must forgive yourself, you are *the only one* who can issue the order for self-forgiveness and then fill it. I think that the reliance on those outside of your own being to do this can keep you from doing it yourself, *for yourself.*

"After I spent the morning engaged in this soul-cleansing ritual, other long-forgotten events occurred to me throughout the day. I dealt with what I could and put off taking care of some of the others until the next time I could go back to the bedroom and give them my full attention. I now do this regularly, while I conscientiously make an effort to avoid doing those things that are bound to engender guilt feelings."

In doing the exercise myself, I too learned that you must forgive yourself for past deeds, must learn from them, and learn to be more discriminating in what you feel guilty about. Usually the guilt that mothers feel is piled on old guilts, so you will want to forgive yourself for things that have nothing to do with your children—stealing candy bars from the grocery store when you were eight; hurting your mother's feelings when you were ten. If you were raised as a guilty person, chances are the feelings of remorse you have *really* are disproportionate. One woman, for example, told me that she was raised by a grandmother who really did believe that anything that gave a person pleasure was sinful.

Then compose a motherhood guilt list. If you feel guilty about any of your feelings, such as anger, remind yourself that you cannot control the way you *feel*, only the way you *behave*. If you consider yourself a sinner because you don't always love being a mother and don't like to spend time with your children, color those feelings normal and take them off the guilty list. An extreme example of guilt over a so-called sin of omission is the mother who told me she felt guilty that she didn't floss the teeth of her two children, who were both under the age of three. She explained that her family dentist told her this was "absolutely necessary" to insure that her children did not develop gum problems later in life. He didn't, however, explain how a mother could do this without getting her fingers snapped off. (Which reminds me, suddenly, that many people who pile "shoulds" on mothers seem to hold the view that what we are dealing with are dolls instead of active children with minds of their own. Anyway, if you don't floss your toddlers' teeth, don't feel guilty.)

Along with this self-forgiveness exercise, it is useful to think about some of the external events and situations that may have undermined your self-esteem. Bring them out into the open. Look at them. Deal with them.

Go all the way back—beyond your motherhood and adult-hood. I remember, for example, a teacher who humiliated me for talking in class. I can still see her face. *Her* actions were inappropriate—she flew into a rage and pulled me out of my chair and shook me while the other children nervously giggled—but *I* felt worthless and extremely guilty. Years later, one of my classmates spread lies about me, nearly ruining my reputation. Even though *I* knew they were lies, somehow just having them said made me feel bad about myself. It was as if there were something bad *in me* that had made the girl act this way. As is true with most of us, I have experienced through the years a number of external shame-making incidents. Remembering them and seeing that they were wrongdoings of others helps us to understand the sorts of things that have got us where we are today in the esteem department.

Something that engenders maternal guilt or makes that which exists even more acute is the confident mother. The very fact that she walks among us causes some of us who aren't confident to feel that there is something inherently wrong with us. But the confident, relatively guilt-free mother is no *better* than the one who suffers from deep feelings of inadequacy. She is just luckier. Perhaps she was imbued with confidence from the day of her birth, given many advantages, and endowed with above-average looks and intelligence. She may have started off her mothering not only with a good sense of who she was but with success at natural childbirth and breastfeeding (or a healthy acceptance of "failure" at either of these must-do's). From the beginning there may have been such advantages as a regular baby nurse, or her mother may have been happy to come in and teach, help, and take over and give her breathing spells. Perhaps she had an unusually supportive and helpful husband; perhaps one that fully shared from the moment of birth. But whatever—I repeat—the confident mother is one very *lucky* woman and not necessarily a paragon of *virtue*.

Less fortunate mothers sometimes reach a point where they lose perspective about just what is worthy of their remorse. A self-assured mother may be able to laugh off trivial failures, but the mother who feels inadequate is more inclined to see all failures in the same light. She may, for example, feel the same degree of guilt for something over which she has no control and isn't necessarily damaging (such as failure at breastfeeding) as when she shakes a fussy baby in a moment of rage. As one mother said, "It all mixes together, the big sins, the small sins, the in-between sins—and becomes an enormous glob."

Thus, I think it is *useful to decide to allot only a reasonable amount of guilt to each specific sort of transgression.* You can start out by dividing them into categories of "Things over which I have no control," and "Things I can control." On the first list, you might put birth complications, poor health, or other acts of God—make your own list. You *do* have control over whether you take good care of your child, and how you act on your feelings. If you don't, for example, feed a child when he's hungry, or you let one wear a wet diaper all day, those sins of omission would go on the second list.

A third category could be things you don't do for your child that you feel you *should* but that aren't essential to his or her well-being. An example might be not mending or ironing baby clothes or, with an older child, not playing games with him or her or being involved in their activities.

Doing Good to Feel Good

Freedom from guilt and having a high level of self-esteem means, to me, not feeling guilty over things that really aren't important, not being crippled by past guilts—but hanging onto them just enough so that they serve as a reminder of not wanting to feel that way again, not subjecting yourself to external guilt and inadequacy-generating situations, and knowing that you cannot go back and undo that which has been done—that yesterday is a cancelled check.

So what can be done about today and tomorrow? One way to start building a healthy self-image might be to make a list of all your good qualities (you probably have more than you might think). It might start out like this:

My Good Points

- I really do love my children
- I want to be a good parent and work toward that goal.
- I do many things for the children every day. (List them.)
- I try to be fair and understanding.
- I resist the impulse to spank them when they don't really deserve it.

You might add to your list qualities that are not necessarily related to parenthood—such as honesty, willingness to help others, kindness, diligence at work.

Next, list what you see as your inadequacies. For example:

My Bad Points

- I'm impatient.
- I'm disorganized.
- Sometimes I'm unfair to the children.
- Sometimes I let the kids get away with murder because I don't want to bother disciplining them.
- I don't keep the kids as groomed as I should.

Again, you might want to add qualities that don't relate directly to the children but tend to add to your overall feelings about yourself.

When you've completed your lists, change "My Bad Points" to read, "Points that Need Working on." Now, arrange each one in the order in which it can be improved upon with the least amount of effort, taking the least amount of time. Take the first one, estimate how long you think it might take you to add it to your list of good points, and then set that as your first goal.

When you have successfully met a goal, reward yourself. Having a cup of coffee and indulging in a TV show in midafternoon or buying a new lipstick might be appropriate for a small success. A medium success could be rewarded with allowing yourself the time to read a book you've been dying to read, while a large success might just warrant something new to wear. However, I feel that the best reward of all is treating yourself to some time for yourself, perhaps to go out to lunch with a friend—not guiltily, but with an attitude that you deserve this day because you have done something worthwhile for yourself and your family.

As you achieve more successes, you will build up your confidence and keep it moving constantly upward. Other ways you can feel good about yourself are to reinforce your strong points by doing tasks that you can do with ease and that make you feel better about yourself. Or, doing things you really should do but keep putting off. Here are some suggestions just to get you started thinking:

- Clean out a drawer, straighten a closet, reorganize one of the kitchen cupboards; clean out your garage.

- Write a long overdue letter; put photos in a photo album.

- Make a list of three tasks to perform in one week's time and then perform them. But don't set up anything that will prove formidable and will take all your time.

- If you feel guilty because you don't read stories to your children, read them a *short* story.

- Don't wait until you feel guilty for being overdue in setting up medical and dental appointments for the children. Just pick up the phone and set them up.

- If there's a tea party at the nursery school or your first-grader is in a play, but you'd rather stay home and watch TV, skip the TV and make *yourself* feel good while you make *your child* feel good.

- Start the day out as right as you can. Sleeping late is, to me, a lousy trade-off for the bad feelings that come if I don't give the children a good start in the morning. I have long recognized that the well-balanced breakfast they get nurtures my sense of well-being every bit as much as it nourishes my children. Lisa and Adam may think I have always crawled out of bed early in the morning for *them,* but I know I do it for *me.* (Some people, by the way, have told me that I'm creating dependency in the children. The hell with them. I disagree and I care more about my self-esteem than someone's else's good opinion of me.)

- Do something you do well but haven't done for a while. If, for example, you bake a fine apple pie, bake one.

- If you have sewing skills, sew something. It doesn't have to be something major that would be difficult to do around the children.

Building Self-Esteem Through Compensation

Dr. James R. Dobson, in his book, *Hide or Seek,* very strongly recommends that parents who wish to help their children develop self-confidence look around for activities that will compensate for "inadequacy" in specific areas. He insists that all children are able to do *something* well, and that, for example, a homely child may be able to compensate—if given the opportunity—by playing a musical instrument.[1] Well, if this works, and I think it does, for children who feel less adequate than their more socially successful peers, surely it can work for mothers who cannot function perfectly as such is decreed, and who thus have come to feel inadequate. Being a supermom, while dubious in any case, isn't the only avenue for the building of self-esteem.

Without discounting the importance to a mother and her children of doing those things for children that are necessary for their well-being and avoiding guilt-making situations, there are areas where we can all do well and thus feel much better about ourselves as individuals. And every bit of confidence helps. One woman, for example, takes voice lessons simply because she has always wanted to. She has come along well enough so that she performs at public recitals and is proud of herself. Another woman I know took up the piano and now plays well enough to feel a sense of accomplishment. Still another, whose children are in school, has returned to school herself. There are many ways in which a woman can reinforce her self-esteem by compensating. You know the ways for yourself. So think about what you might want to do and set about finding ways—as you might for your child—to do them. Drawing, painting, gourmet cooking, music, crafts, a job outside the home—whatever. Remember, you need not be Michelangelo or Van Cliburn to know the feeling of accomplishment. And know this: *perfect is the enemy of good.* The goal of perfection in any endeavor virtually guarantees failure; the idea that perfect is necessary or desirable can keep people from even trying to do anything tolerably well. And know and remember this too: *don't forget the value of redirecting the energy of your anger into positive and constructive activity.*

For mothers who have the time or who can make arrangements to have it, one good use of energy can be volunteer work, which can be most reinforcing—you can feel good about yourself for making a worthwhile contribution to the community, and often there are projects involving more than stuffing envelopes that are stimulating and remind you, if you are a housewife, that you are capable of doing something beyond housework and taking care of children. And, of course, built into most volunteer jobs is the opportunity to meet people and make new friends.

However, some women tell me that they feel they shouldn't do volunteer work because a couple of years back, leaders of the National Organization for Women said they shouldn't—the theory being that first, if a job is worthwhile, a person should get paid for doing it, and next, that when women did volunteer work, it perpetuated the low status of women. I'm not sure I agree with that. I am sure, however, that it is antithetical to the cause of freedom or liberation for the movement or any of its spokespersons to tell others how they *should* conduct their personal lives—there is no place for *shoulds* in *any* liberation movement. People ought to have the freedom to do those things that are not harmful to other people and that help them to feel good without feeling guilty or receiving criticism. Just as I feel it is unwise for a mother to sacrifice herself for her family, I do not go along with a philosophy of doing "anything for the cause," if that "anything" involves either personal sacrifice or a conflict in fundamental values—or, in the case at hand, *not* doing something you'd like to do because some volunteer in the National Organization for Women said that you shouldn't do volunteer work.

Sacrificing oneself for the cause brings me to a warning about volunteer work. Remembering that it is vital to be realistic in setting goals for yourself, if you decide to do volunteer work don't take on more than you can comfortably handle. Make it clear from the start the maximum amount of time you can give and stick to your guns. It's amazing how easy it is to find yourself gradually and unconsciously assuming more and more work and then, rather suddenly, becoming overwhelmed—which may defeat the purpose for becoming involved in the first place.

From doing volunteer work myself, I have learned that first, it's easy to replace your need for ego gratification as a mother with that earned by being a volunteer. This is a trap that can interfere with your personal life. Second, I have learned that a lot of pressure is applied to volunteers to do more than they want to do or originally contracted to do, and the primary tool some community project leaders use is laying guilt trips on those who resist. So, I say, never give *a reason* for saying no to additional work. ("I don't want to tell you why" works very well.) Third, it's important not to allow your dinner hour and your evening to be disrupted by phone calls or visits from eager crusaders. Now that you've been warned of some of the pitfalls, if you'd like to find some of the rewards, call your local volunteer bureau or campaign headquarters.

When Your Job Is the Pits

The working mother has been conspicuous by her absence in this chapter. She is by no means neglected, and, in fact, she is the star of the next chapter. However, here I think some consideration of the possible effects of working in a bad job is appropriate to any discussion focusing on self-esteem. I think it's especially appropriate here because a mother doesn't necessarily have to work outside the home to have a bad job.

In any case, when your job makes you feel worthless, it's time to think about getting another one—if at all possible. I once worked as an order clerk in a title insurance company, for example. This dead-end job was so boring and left so little room for innovation that occcasionally I fell asleep at my desk, which didn't do a lot for my self-image. Realizing that I couldn't continue this way, one day, following one of my unintentional naps, I gave notice.

But a "bad job" isn't necessarily just one that is a so-called dead-end job or one that is boring; instead it can be any job that contains elements that rob a person of his or her self-esteem. Many years after resigning from the job that would have been an insomniac's delight, I worked as the executive director of a large national environmental organization. The opportunities for excitement and challenge were seemingly endless. But for all of the superficial ego-reinforcing potential of this particular position, there were too many nonconstructive challenges to both my capability and integrity. I found myself in the unique and untenable position of being under constant scrutiny and being continually on the defensive. The result was the steady erosion of my self-confidence. The day I left this outfit was one of the best days of my life, and I wondered why, when it felt so good to go, it had taken me so long to find the door. The obvious answer is, of course, that the job was prestigious. But surface prestige is no substitute for feeling good—all the way inside— about yourself. This job may have held all sorts of opportunities for glory, but there were *far* more opportunities for making me feel terrible. Who needs it? Especially what *mother*, who has her own separate set of anxiety-producing situations?

After this experience I resolved that nothing could ever keep me in a job that insured that I would daily question my worth. It taught me that to do so made it even more difficult to look elsewhere for work—because it's hard to make a good impression on a prospective employer when you don't bring high self-esteem to the interview. I recognize that there are some mothers who, for financial reasons, seem not to have a choice, but I surely would recommend that, whenever possible, a woman in a situation like the one I was in, seriously consider a job change.

In between the job that put me to sleep and the one that made me so anxious that getting a good night's rest was impossible were ten years' worth of good working experiences—the sort of experiences that make people feel good, not just because of the work but because of the people. In contrasting my ten good years with the rotten six months in the title company and the even rottener two years with the environmental organization (where many of the people were truly pigs), I have come to feel that whether you work or not, people who make you feel lousy— whom you either actively dislike or who harass or criticize you without warrant—are not and cannot ever be your friends and you really ought to have as little to do with them as possible.

Self-Esteem and Self-Care

To be effective, any program for building self-esteem must include the decision to be good to yourself—to treat yourself as you feel a worthwhile person deserves to be treated. And that means that there is no place for self-destructive behavior in your plan. I said, for example, that I get up early to get my children off to a good start every day because it makes me feel good about myself. But I should add that to be able to do this requires that I get enough sleep. In fact, to do most of the reinforcing things I do—from taking care of my family to doing the work that is my very own, I have to take care of myself. That includes getting proper rest, eating nutritious foods, keeping the vices (coffee, alcohol, tobacco) in relative moderation, and having regular medical and dental exams.

My mental health is sustained by having balance in my life (admittedly, I'm not always as successful as I'd like to be with this, but it's a goal I continue to work toward). To obtain that balance, I bow to no dogmas, but instead do what feels right for me after spending several hours at the typewriter each day—

and that could be baking cookies with the children or doing hand-sewing. And I really don't give a damn if those things that make me feel good are so-called stereotypic activities. Seeing friends, reading, going to the movies once in a while, taking in a concert, swimming and playing Frisbee—and even watching TV—while not functional in conventional (guilt-making) terms, can give life balance. Balance is loving family life, good and reinforcing work...and fun.

You *are* worthy and deserving. And that means that unless you commit heinous crimes against the state or individuals, you absolutely are not for kicking. Not by your husband, your children, or anyone else. Especially, not by yourself.

8
Guilt and the Working Mother

There are mothers who work outside the home who feel no guilt whatsoever about that fact of their lives. I am aware of the existence of at least four of them. In contrast, I know dozens of working mothers who feel guilty and who worry about whether they are so depriving their children that Leavenworth may be the alternative institution to the university when the kids reach college age. Backing up those I know personally are many mothers I've never met, but feel I know through the tortured letters they've written to me. Thus, I've concluded that if guilt is built into the motherhood role generally, working mothers experience it even more intensely than mothers who stay home with their children.

Sadly, the women's movement notwithstanding, society does decree that a woman's place is in the home. It is a strong tradition that we live with—strong because it has been with us from the time we were little girls watching our mother's mother, and strong because it is totally reinforced in all of the media. Even those of us who may truly believe that a woman's place is in the *world* are subject, on a nearly reflexive basis, to the guilt and fear that grow out of the foundation of traditionalism.

That tradition is still with us, and strongly so, can be seen in the need to defend doing that which is "untraditional." So, we are now saying more and more that it's *good* for mother and *good* for her children if mother works outside the home for fulfillment. While that may be true when that's the case, the implication is that all mothers work for fulfillment. And that leads detractors of working mothers to come back with suggestions that most mothers who work do so for purely hedonistic reasons.

The fact is, *most* people do *not* work for fulfillment, but instead for *money*. And the high cost of raising a family all too often means that no matter what an individual woman's or a couple's personal philosophy may be, a mother is likely to find herself in the work force. A survey in *The New York Times* on "The Changing American Family" clearly stated, "Of the various reasons propelling mothers into business and industry, family finances are usually a major consideration." Most women, the survey noted, usually cite specific material goals as the reason they work, in addition to supplementing inadequate wages brought home by the husband.[1]

Who says mothers shouldn't work? Who says mothers work only for fulfillment? The middle ground of reality does get lost between the old and new myths, doesn't it? And we know who gets caught in the crunch, don't we?

However. I *do* admit that some women work not just for bread alone—some really enjoy working, some are dedicated to a particular profession, and some would rather work than stay home all day with their children. There are even mothers who are driven from their homes because they are being made berserk by their children and the horribly impossible role that traditional motherhood has imposed. And they feel guilty as hell. Guilty for *being* away, of course, but guiltier still for *wanting* to be away. Because, weirdly, in this culture that doesn't readily acknowledge that mothers do sometimes need to work for money, there co-exists the notion that when they *do* work, *normal* mothers would rather stay home and wipe noses and referee sparring matches between siblings. And thus any mother who feels otherwise is some sort of a monster.

One such "monster" I talked to is Nan, the mother of three. She tried staying home for a while, but when her second child was two years old, she returned to work fulltime. After a brief maternity leave to have her third child eight years ago, Nan returned to her job and has been there ever since. As she explains it, after staying home with the first two for as long as she did, she knew, at some level of consciousness, that she would go stark raving mad if she had to be home with the children, Mr. Rogers, and the Cookie Monster all day, every day. She says that it took her a while to realize that being at home would do her in. "A mother has a hard time admitting such things to herself," she said. "It was far easier for me to tell myself that I *wanted* to work than it would have been to admit to such unmotherly feelings as wanting to be away from the children—*wanting* to work was bad enough.

"And then," she continued, "besides my guilt over not wanting to be with the kids all the time, I have nagging fears that my working and being away is going to hurt my kids."

Is Working Harmful to Your Children?

Nan typifies the working mother who truly gets it from all sides, which is perhaps why she worries about what her working is doing to her children. And that she is sensitive about working is perhaps why she is easy prey for disapproving friends, relatives, schoolteachers, and nonworking mothers—more so than those four confident, guilt-free working mothers I know. And all of the criticism that Nan receives reinforces her fundamental fear that her working is going to prove to be damaging to her children, whom she does indeed genuinely love.

Because of the hard time Nan and dozens of women who have talked to me or sent me letters have been given by preschool and elementary schoolteachers (some of whom seem to delight in putting the screws to working mothers), I should probably devote an entire chapter to schools. But being the very soul of restraint, I'll keep it down to a few paragraphs. At least for now. I have one very fat folder of letters from working mothers who say they are constantly made to feel as if their children are being genuinely deprived, if not out-and-out dangerously neglected because they work and do not have the time to participate in school activities. I know that the guilt I felt at not baking brownies to sell at the carnival was more deeply felt than was appropriate because of the pressure put on me by room-mothers. But that pressure was nothing to the telephone calls in the evening (while I was trying to get dinner together) from my son's teacher, admonishing me for not patching the holes in his jeans or for letting his hair get a trifle too long for her standards. Her words during one of our conversations still ring in my ears: "Don't you think you ought to set aside your own interests for these few years when your baby needs you?"

Teachers, and other people infected by the school system, have an uncanny flair for engendering guilt in mothers—for implying that working is evidence of disinterest, leads children to fail in school, and creates feelings of insecurity. And the fact that just about *anyone* affiliated with a school is often seen as an expert on children makes their views particularly persuasive.

What fascinates me the most about teachers and other employees in schools laying trips on working mothers is that many of them *are working mothers themselves*. The message I get is that it's okay to work if you work with children—whether or not the children are yours—but not okay to work in another field. Unless, of course, you *really* must work to put food on the table. That is, it's okay for mom to work if the alternatives are either starvation or welfare. I fail to understand the reasoning behind the idea that children won't suffer if mother *must* work, but that they will if she *chooses* to.

There is absolutely no evidence to support the notion that children are damaged or deprived because their mothers work. When she was a professor of Pediatrics and Associate Dean of Harvard Medical School, Dr. Mary Howell* surveyed 280 reports in the literature and concluded that the children of working mothers fared just as well as those of mothers who stayed home all day. Another study, conducted in 1970, by Dr. Mary Elizabeth Keister, of the University of North Carolina, revealed that day-care children she studied from birth to five years were, if anything, slightly ahead of their peers who were exclusively reared by their parents. She also found that in physical and emotional development the children she studied showed no differences from their peers who were cared for exclusively by their parents.[2]

In fact, numerous studies[3] show that not only are children not damaged when their mothers work, but they are likely to be well socialized if they go to preschool groups, and are apt to be independent and make good adjustments when they enter regular school. *Try as I might, I could not find one single study focused on average families that supported the old wives' tale that children are better off when mom stays home.*

At a more personal level, I do not know of a single child who has been damaged because his or her mother worked—and I know working mothers whose children cover virtually every age range. What I have observed, however, is that working

---

*Currently Education and Evaluation Coordinator, Geriatrics Research Educational and Clinical Center, Bedford Medical Center, Bedford, Massachusetts.

mothers are very conscientious about their children. Consider the working mother, an executive secretary, who said, "If I didn't have this good job, I'd scrub floors at night to pay for having the kids' teeth straightened," or the cleaning woman I know who did just that so her four children could have the advantage of college educations.

When the disapproval and guilt are generously dished out, the working mother who absorbs it is laboring under the illusion that *all* mothers who stay home *always* do many things for their children. If you are a working mother, while you are castigating yourself, try to remember that your perceptions of what all homemakers actually do all day may be completely out of whack. Sure, some mothers are very involved with their children, but some are not. And some are so sick and tired of being with kids all the time that they just can't get up the energy to do as much with or for them as the average working mother does with hers. And remember, too, that some mothers who are trapped in the house are falling apart at the seams (which I suspect is far more hazardous to the mental well-being of their children than having sane working mothers might be). And those of celebrity who get up and preach about where a woman's place is frequently don't spend much time there themselves—examples that come all too quickly to mind are Phyllis Schlafly and Marabel Morgan.

When Old and New Myths Collide

Either I read somewhere, or some young dewy-eyed feminist said to me, that mothers are refreshed when they come home to their children after being out in the working world. Just the idea makes me hysterical. *Refreshed?* How in the world could anyone be *refreshed* after putting in a long day at work and coming home to the demands of the family. How many *refreshed* working fathers do you know? My husband surely isn't one of them—he practically crawls into the house on all fours when he comes home from work. And he loves his job, which should put him way ahead in the refreshment department. How many people—how many mothers in particular—can say they truly love their work? An additional advantage, which he and other fathers have that working mothers do not have, is that he isn't carrying around a huge sackful of guilt over working outside the home.

The reason I don't like the myth that women are *refreshed* from working all day is, first, it isn't always true, and, next, it puts some of the more truthful statements that have come out of the women's movement in more questionable light. For example, children don't suffer because their mothers work. This is not a myth, but the notion of fulfilling work leaving women refreshed obscures the fact that while children don't suffer, mothers themselves frequently are another matter. Many do indeed suffer. I know that Nan does, and in her off hours she is one of the most conscientious mothers I know, but still she berates herself for not having the patience to be with her young children all day. And consider the remarks of this woman who works not to get away but out of dedication to her profession— which *is* a fulfilling one:

For years I have struggled with the guilt of leaving my children to do my work. I have told myself that it can be done—indeed I need to do it and I make a contribution. And yet, I'm torn. I'm two people. My identity constantly undergoes daily dramatic changes. The worst of it is that I feel like I'm doing a lousy job both at home and in my medical practice. I don't think this conflict will be resolved until the children are grown. Already I have regrets about not spending enough time with them, and I know that once they are grown and gone I'll live with the guilt and regret for the rest of my life. I am a doctor. I can't not be. I am also a mother. I can't not be that either.

And let us not forget that the routine of the average working mother isn't exactly a lark. Besides dealing with feelings of guilt, it sometimes seems to take the combined efforts of an efficiency expert and a mystic just to keep all the arrangements in working order. This, from a mother who seems disturbed at the clash between maternal reality and proposals for liberating mothers:

Being a working mother is not easy. I have an otherwise intelligent twenty-one-year-old sister who is a sophomore...and who (along with her friends) believes that the problem with us pre-liberation mothers is that we have a "hang-up" about our kids needing us. She and her friends are going to have zingy professions, just like men, free from guilt. They aren't particularly interested in hearing that (a) children have a way of making you feel responsible for them, and (b) even if they don't, those terrific free community-controlled twenty-four-hour-a-day care centers or even reasonable facsimiles of same haven't been built yet, so you're stuck with the responsibility all the same.

I'm often in the position, particularly with younger feminists, of being held up as an example of a woman who has it all. On the surface, it's true—I have two nice kids and a good job. But I often worry that I'm doing a half-assed job at both ends, and even when things are going well I find that it requires extraordinary energy just to keep all the arrangements in working order. (God forbid that it's Martin Luther King Day and no school, or that somebody's sick, or that I have to work overtime.)...I wish more women would speak out on this. It only oppresses our sisters if we pretend that being superwomen is possible or even desirable.

One woman who did speak out publicly, to United Press International, suffered enough from being a working mother so that she retreated. A mother of two and an interior designer, she said that the four roles she played—wife, mother, homemaker, and career woman—for two-and-one-half years had exhausted her both physically and emotionally. "You can only play the roles for so long," she said, "without something happening...Being a perfectionist, I couldn't split myself in those ways."[4]

One does not have to be a perfectionist to experience a certain amount of schizophrenia at functioning in four separate and demanding roles. Not every working mother goes through this, but many do. And they say it is difficult to make the transition from office to home—that it is a dramatic one for them, and that there is really no time to shift gears. I do recall what it was like for me when I worked in an office. I remember coming home, often with work still on my mind; setting down my briefcase, hanging up my coat, and putting on an apron, all rather automatically while I halfway listened to the sitter tell me what had gone on and had a vague sense of lots of little hands pulling at my skirt. It was like culture shock. Often I wasn't completely clear on just what it was I was supposed to be doing. Oddly enough, until I talked to other working mothers about this, I thought I was unique, which of course led to the distinct feeling that I was incompetent.

Contributing to the anguish I have felt as a working mother—whether I was working in an office or working at home as I'm doing at this moment—has been the sense that other working mothers manage so much better than I. After I had written about the difficulties in combining a career with motherhood, the problems in finding good child care, and my feelings of guilt over not spending enough time with the children, I received a letter from a mother who wanted to let me know just where I'd gone wrong. One paragraph stands out in my mind:

Both my husband and I teach at the university here, and we have arranged our schedules so that one of us is always home to care for our three-year-old daughter. If more couples would work out similar arrangements, they could manage as well as we do.

Some of my best friends are in academia. Some of them, however, have a surprisingly limited view of the rest of the world. A professor of mathematics I know, for example, is married to a woman in technical management in the electronics industry. As do most other people in similar occupations (like my own husband), she works at least forty hours a week. Since this man spends only six hours at the university each week, he has concluded—and he's not joking—that his wife has a neurotic compulsion about work, which is why she spends so much time there. He works at home much of the time, so why can't she? Well, she just can't—not if she wants to hang on to her job, that is.

And even on those rare occasions when people can work out arrangements whereby one parent is always at home, it isn't always as wonderful for everyone as the stories would lead us to believe.

There does exist much evidence that, *in most cases,* the ties that bind are stronger between mothers and children, even when mothers would like to be away, than between fathers and children. I have read all the words. I have seen fathers change diapers, and I know some who get up in the night with crying infants. I know two who share totally, and I'm aware of the existence of house-husbands, and I even know one. I also know a divorced father who has custody of his daughter, another who would like to have custody of his three boys, and a single man who adopted two boys. But however much I may endorse the idea of fathers being fully committed to their children, as mothers generally are, I know these men to be exceptions rather than the general rule. I have not seen widespread and dramatic changes, generally, in the parenthood setup in the last ten years. A handful of sharing and nurturing fathers doesn't knock out the very real fact that most of the time the buck stops with mother, *not* with father.

Mothers can argue long and hard that it isn't fair and not sensible that they are so totally responsible for the children, as most are, but blueprints for egalitarian arrangements do not take into account the feelings and reflexes of mothers, or the cultural realities with which we all are living. For example, what would happen if the school nurse called father at his office. How would a *typical* father respond? Quite likely he would be rather taken aback and tell the nurse to call his wife and give her the phone number (if he remembers what it is). But then, the school nurse wouldn't call father in the first place, unless, of course she'd already tried to reach mother and couldn't get her. When mother *is* reached, how does she respond? Quite a bit differently, I'd say, from your average father. Virtually every mother I know would respond initially to such a dreaded call with a stab of fear—icy fingers closing in on her heart, panic. If the child is merely ill and not dying or already dead, the next response, after collecting her wits, is to go over to the school and pick up her sick child and take him or her home. If the child has a broken leg, and this time it is the nurse at the day-care center or the baby-sitter who calls mother at her office, mother is likely to feel some irrational guilt—that things like this wouldn't happen to her children if she didn't work. How many *fathers* ever feel that way? It is only later that a mother might be able to reason that children fall out of trees all the time when their mothers *are at home.* And it is very much later that she may question why it is always *she* who gets called away when a child needs a parent.

And what about when the baby is ill in the morning and both parents are getting ready to go to work? Who is more likely to stay home with the baby? The father of a sick child can manage to keep his mind on his work, but no mother with a heart can leave a sick child with someone else—not even, in some cases, her own husband—and then give her full attention to her job.

Not only do many mothers feel more responsible for the welfare of their children, but children naturally gravitate toward their mothers. Even when fathers are available and willing to see to their needs, it is mother whom the children bring their scraped knees and wounded vanities.

It is wise to encourage them to take their hurts to their fathers, and wise to encourage fathers to step in—I've done so for years and, obviously, I urge others to do so as well—but we cannot *force* fathers and children to change. Whatever causes the symbiosis that exists between mothers and children generally—whether it is biological or conditioned—it would take a monumental effort to undo it, and another monumental effort to turn fathers into mothers. To have as a goal *complete* reversal in the conditioning of men and women is unrealistic, in most cases, and can set us up for new frustrations, resentments, and more feelings of inadequacy at our failure to accomplish this.

And I think that the idea that the egalitarian dream can be carried off with ease and intelligent scheduling if most mothers work part time or have flexible schedules diminishes the efforts and accomplishments of those mothers who work full time outside the home and manage to be relatively efficient at home and relatively involved with their children.

I also think that the misapprehension that it is easier than it actually is for most working mothers could, if allowed to exist, perpetuate itself to such an extent that what few support systems there are for working mothers might dwindle. Especially when the idea that it is easy combines with the idea that mothers work mostly for fulfillment. "If it's all that easy, and these gals work for fun," snorts Senator Littlemind, "then why the hell should we appropriate any money for day-care centers?"

When any style of motherhood is generalized, myths are made. And myths cause people to have high expectations of what they actually can do—and those who can't meet a given standard, old or new, wind up feeling frustrated, disappointed, and inadequate. Very real problems get ignored along the way. How much, for example, might some of the contemporary high-flown ideas have contributed to the problems of that woman who spoke frankly to United Press about her inability to cope with her compartmentalized life? It might not have solved her problems had she realized that her conflicts were not unique, but it might have been comforting had she known that she was by no means alone. What if the literature we're all exposed to, instead of featuring women who have worked out the logistics beautifully, more often dealt with women who experience the conflicts as both painful and normal and stages that don't last forever? Just the knowledge that as the children got older they wouldn't need so much attention and care might have given her a glimmer of hope—and the glimmer might have helped her to cope with the confusion and work out better arrangements for all of the domestic duties that so overwhelmed her. Perhaps she would have been moved to wonder why, even though she was working full time, the burden of all the housework still fell on her shoulders alone.

Housework, Guilt, and the Working Mother

It was in the early sixties that I worked for a large corporation. I was married but as yet had no children, which was not the case for many of the women I worked with. The working mother, contrary to current rhetoric, is not a new invention. Most of the women I worked with were mothers and all of them were working because they needed the money.

Jane, the mother of four children, described her daily routine this way: up at the crack of dawn, she would make breakfast for the family, get the children dressed, get herself dressed, and then take the children to the sitter's, getting to work as close to eight as possible. After working all day, she'd leave the office, pick up the children, drive home, start dinner, start trying to reduce the mountain of dirty laundry that four children and two adults can generate, eat, supervise the children, and clean up the dinner dishes. Once the children were in bed, Jane either did some housework or some ironing, and would fall in bed at about midnight. She was always exhausted, and it showed— dark circles under her tired eyes, shoulders always hunched. But she never questioned that this was the price she had to pay for being a working mother—even though the reason she worked was that her husband didn't earn enough money to support the family.

Frances usually worked six days a week—partly because the job frequently called for it and partly because with three children to raise, she and her husband could always use the extra money. However, she often became enraged at the way "their" extra money got spent—on power tools, water-ski gear, and green fees on the golf course. And she carried with her a seething resentment that she spent her days off cleaning house, while her husband Bruce spent *his* playing golf. He was tired, he said, from working all week and deserved a little relaxation. One can only guess that Frances was seen as some sort of machine that could go on endlessly. They fought bitterly, but nothing ever changed, and I was left with the impression that the marriage would end before any changes in Bruce's attitude or Frances's routine would occur. When Frances would rage, her husband Bruce would retaliate by calling her a shrew and a nag—incapable of having any fun or allowing anyone else to have any fun.

There were dozens of other working mothers with stories similar to those of Jane and Frances. But Marsha's was typical of that period. Marsha had become pregnant shortly after she and her husband were married, and in those days there really was little anyone could do about an unplanned pregnancy except have the baby. So Marsha had her baby boy and when he was three months old, she made arrangements for child care and returned to her job. Her husband was going to medical school, and seeing that he got through it and became a doctor was their shared goal. So, every morning without fail, Marsha got up at five-thirty, got herself dressed for work, dressed and fed the baby, took him off to the baby-sitter's, and went on to her job. At the end of the day, she'd pick up the baby, rush home, prepare dinner, feed the baby, and catch up on the laundry and housework, all this while making sure that the baby didn't cry—everything had to be nice and quiet so that her husband, the Future Doctor, could study. And then one day this man, motioning in the direction of a chair in their bedroom that was about to collapse under the weight of the clothes he'd routinely dumped on it, said to his wife, "Can't you at least hang up my clothes?" *All* of Marsha's fatigue and restrained anger came out in an ugly explosion which left her feeling guilty. Repentantly, she hung up her husband's clothes.

But that was long ago and times have changed. Women no longer are being forced to carry the entire burden. They've had their consciousnesses raised and they simply won't do it. Well ... not exactly. In May 1978, *Redbook* magazine sponsored a survey that revealed that a *majority* of husbands of working women share the housework a little or not at all, while a scant 12 percent share equally.[5]

But how can that be possible? "My God, is it 1952 and nobody has told us?" asks Cari Beauchamp, the fiery feminist. "This can't be! With so many women returning to work and so many millions of words having been spoken and written in recent years on these issues, it is unbelievable that the percentage of men who presently share equally is probably no greater than it was ten, twenty, thirty years ago."

How can that be possible? Well, to begin with, when a wife works and there are no children, it is easy for her to slip into the habit of doing everything, partly because she's been pro-grammed to do so all her life and partly because she wants to please her new husband. And, of course, playing house can be fun at first. When there are no children, there's really not all that much housework. But when children figure in the picture, that's quite another matter; nonetheless the established pat-tern persists, and pretty soon the wife is taking care of the house and the children, even though she may have gone back to work. And gradually the slow and quiet burn begins as working mothers begin to seethe with rage and resentment over the unfairness of it all. Meanwhile, back in the living room, their husbands sit, whining about how their jobs wear them out: "Get me a beer, will you, honey—what a day I've had."

That such a situation can continue long after it should be apparent to those involved that it is wholly unjust tells me that our programming might have been even more extensive than we think. For example, some of us have been programmed not only to be wives and mothers but also to see our husbands as authority figures—bosses, fathers—whose approval we must have and whose disapproval is too painful to risk. For example, I can now identify some of the feelings I had when I went back to work in 1969. Although I was angry over the unfair division of responsibility, whenever I let things slide I felt like I was being judged a misbehaving child—a bad girl trying to get away with something or trying to get out of doing something I was supposed to do. Those feelings were especially acute when I was really hostile and openly rebelling. My feelings, of course, were irrational. But then the whole gestalt is irrational—the exhausted wife, defensive and guilty over not being superwoman and the husband, who professes to love her, seemingly devoid of a grain of empathy (and possibly critical of his wife's efforts).

When I dwell on this situation, the whole question of the role women have traditionally occupied takes on a deeper meaning for me. A component in making us truly subservient is to program us to be *obedient children*. The prevailing societal view has been that we shouldn't work—to do so is to misbehave.

Thus, while some women say it is easier just to do everything themselves, or that trying to get their husbands to share creates too much tension, pride figures in, too. The day has not yet come when the outside influences are there for men, as they are for women. Nobody is going to say of my husband, "My, Cal surely is a rotten housekeeper—and his children run around in such dingy-looking clothes! And would you believe??? He almost *never* irons Shirley's clothes, and the poor thing really has to look nice on the job." And I have yet to hear a schoolteacher scold a father for not making it to an afternoon play, see a Brownie leader shake her head sadly that father didn't make it to the tea party, or the PTA president complain that she can't get enough fathers to bake cakes for the PTA fund-raising bake sale. When men are fulfilling their roles as breadwinners by working and supporting the family, guilt is not heaped on them—because *they* are doing what *they* are supposed to do.

Theories about equality and fair play may have come a long way, but in bypassing a stage of our development through simple ignorance of the child within, some of us have yet to catch up. I think now of a woman I know who writes me long soul-baring letters, the theme of which, repeatedly, is the conflict she feels over working, having three children, and housework. She laments that she has so little time—time to keep the house the way it ought to be kept and the way she feels her husband expects her to. She doesn't always iron his shirts, and she feels guilty. Nor does she wash the windows often enough. Sometimes she only vacuums the house every three weeks or so, which she sees as a sort of disgrace. She seems to work constantly and then feels resentful that she never has any time to herself.

"I could give up sleep, and work around the clock," she writes. "And I still wouldn't catch up—I still wouldn't be able to do anything for myself." On those occasions when she *does* take time out, she feels the need to rationalize it, but winds up saying, "I know I shouldn't have..." She resents it that her husband doesn't share, and resents it even more that it doesn't bother him and that he seems to do whatever he wants to do— without any guilt feelings. Making matters worse is that she feels that he disapproves of her for not getting all the housework done. "Even though I'm killing myself while he sits around, I feel guilty—which is crazy."

Carefully and sequentially rereading the letters this woman has written me, I see pieces start to fall into place and form a picture. The pressure my friend feels to do absolutely every-thing is *self-inflicted.* Perhaps her husband doesn't share be-cause she's never asked him to. Perhaps it doesn't occur to him to do so voluntarily because all of these things aren't important to him—at least not to the degree that they are to her. Perhaps the disapproval she senses in him is the disapproval she would feel (and does) because the standards she has set for herself are rooted in her need not to be seen as lazy or sloppy. It is just possible that my friend's husband views the whole housecleaning scene and interacting with the children as *her trip*—while she's seething with guilt and resentment, he may feel that she is merely quietly doing the things she likes to do. And that's not an unusual assumption to make if most of the other working married mothers he knows are also being driven by the same forces.

"Sugar and spice and everything nice." And clean. Good girls are clean. If they aren't clean, they ought to be ashamed of themselves. If they don't do what they're supposed to do, they ought to be ashamed of themselves. So, we are proud of ourselves when we are clean, and proud of ourselves when we do what we're supposed to do. We are even prouder when we do more than can be easily managed—without help from others ("Please, Mother, I'd rather do it myself"). Consider, for example, the way we might view two successful working mothers whose situations are identical except that one has a full-time housekeeper: "Mary is truly remarkable—she holds down a full-time job and does all her own housework. Jan? Oh, yes, she's most successful, but why shouldn't she be, what with all that help she has?"

Complicating matters even more, I suspect, is the fact that some women are truly in conflict over relinquishing certain aspects of the traditional role. Even though we may be exhausted and outwardly wish to be relieved of most responsibilities, we can feel a pull. Do some of us, I wonder, unconsciously fear that relinquishing control over certain of our jobs will lead to some sort of takeover of what little power we have? Perhaps we fear that a part of our identity will be stripped from us. Do we worry that we will no longer be the center of our households? Ridiculous, to be sure. But then hanging on to all our chores and not asking for help when we are worn to a nub is ridiculous too.

Steps that Can Lighten the Housekeeping Burden

To begin with, we mothers must be utterly truthful and very grown-up about why we are willing to work ourselves into our respective frazzles. We must then resolve to stop being "obedient children" and get our egos out of our housework and take deeper pride in other of our strong points and accomplishments. We must ask ourselves if we are aspiring to be superwomen, and, if that's a possibility, remind ourselves that the rewards of that are exhaustion and anger. We must work to get rid of the guilty pride that keeps us "behaving" and resentfully scrubbing floors, and if we can't get rid of it, we must vigorously ignore it.

Some husbands may want to help, but every time they start to do something, their wives take over. To protect their territories? Because they can do it faster? Because they are conditioned? Whatever, if we wish to be freed from the heavy burden of all or most of the household chores, I say when he starts to do something, *leave it alone!* Don't question it. Let him do it. Let him botch it up—he'll get the idea and if he needs help or instruction, he'll let you know. And when *you* need help, asking directly gets better results than silent suffering and telling him with your body language that you hate his guts.

There is another hang-up, often expressed by working wives, when they see their husbands taking out the garbage or getting out the vacuum cleaner—defensiveness when they think there is some hidden message in a sudden interest in domesticity. A friend of mine tells this story:

It always just annoyed me no end that Bob never did anything around the house. I did it all and a sparkling home was something he seemed to take for granted. And that annoyed me even more—that he never seemed to realize that I put a real effort into it. I recall once when I was washing windows I became absolutely irate about his cavalier attitude. And then, a few months later, when I was taking some classes and didn't have much time, I stopped being the paragon of homemaking virtue I'd always been. We were sitting on the patio one day—I was studying—when Bob suddenly said, "My God, look at those windows—they are abso-

lutely opaque!" I took that as a criticism but returned to my work—seething, of course. And so unnecessarily! About an hour later, there stood Bob, washing the windows. And not at all unhappily! He didn't do it to make a statement but because he noticed that the windows were dirty. It was then that I realized that I'd always kept up things so well that nothing that needed to be done stood out. The lesson I've learned is threefold—not to be so damn efficient about the house, not to interfere when Bob starts working on something, and not take his actions as his way of telling me that I'm not doing my job.

Before we can know for sure whether our husbands are willing to share part of the burden, we first must let them know that the burden exists—it may actually not be as obvious as we think it is. At the same time we have to be willing to let them help. If it turns out that we're still stuck with *all* the crappy jobs, then we can decide whether we want to wear ourselves out and be angry a lot of the time while endlessly debating the issue with our husbands, or *do* something concrete to improve the situation for ourselves.

The ideal setup, of course (whether a husband is willing to share or not), for every dual-career family is hiring a house-keeper who will take care of the children. But that being out of reach financially for most of us, the next best thing is taking the kids to a sitter and hiring someone to come in and clean the house.

A feminist argument I've heard against having domestic help is that paying someone else to clean your house is perpetuating the oppression of other women, and demeaning them when you hire them as "servants." What is this, anyway? Consciousness-raising through deprivation of wages? And besides, who says you have to hire *women?* There are numerous house-cleaning services listed in the Yellow Pages and the classified sections of the newspapers that employ *both* sexes to clean residences as well as offices. And those who do the actual work—men *or* women—do not take very kindly to other folks calling their honest work "demeaning."

As an aside, if you look upon house-cleaning as a lowly job, there's the chance you will convey that lack of respect to the people who might do it for you. If, on the other hand, you recognize the value of those who might constitute part of your support system—that is, respect their expertise and appreciate that it allows *you* to do your job, and say so—everyone benefits.

Another feminist dogma that might hang you up is one that holds that *you* shouldn't have to make the arrangements for child care and other outside services—that *men* should be equally involved in this, calling when it's their turn to call. Doubtless that's true. But I don't have the energy for this sort of purist nit-picking. I'd rather make the arrangements than waste my time, my breath, and my creative energy persuading my husband that he should do this, and then explain precisely what needs to be done to him so that he can explain it to someone else. Political nit-picking is a luxury, I think, reserved for the leisure class, of which I am decidedly not a member.

My advice to any working mother who is overwhelmed with guilt, child care, worry, and drudgery, is to take some time to catch her breath at the very first opportunity. Tell your employer that you need two days off to take care of some personal business—which is true enough. Then be sure you have child care (preferably outside the home) lined up. And then take one day and look at your routine and see what you can do to reduce the amount of time you must spend on it.

- Make a list of household chores. Which of them can you pay someone else to do for you? Which, such as polishing silver, are not vital to maintaining reasonable cleanliness and order?

- What errands do you run? Which of these could be accomplished with a phone call and a delivery service? The laundry and dry cleaners? The pharmacy? How much time can you save by letting your fingers do the walking—calling ahead to determine if a store has what you intend to purchase there?

- What things could you get your husband to do without arguing with him so long that it would cancel out any time you might save? Pay the household bills? Do the grocery shopping? (Some men really like to do this for some strange reason.) Does he perhaps harbor a secret desire to take up gourmet cooking? He should by all means be encouraged to pursue such an interest.

After you've made a reasonable assessment of how you can climb out of a horrendously demanding maintenance routine, then make as many arrangements as possible. *By phone!*

Buying services buys you time for yourself and time to spend with the family. It clears out enough of the fuzziness and confusion so that you can think constructively about what is really important—dealing with your feelings, your needs, and your children, and how all of that interrelates.

Spending Time with Your Children

Once we mothers are able to overcome—or, at least come to grips with—our conditioning, or whatever it is that drives us, we can separate the issue of the unfair housekeeping arrangements from the more real, important, human isssues. In other words, the guilt of the obedient-child floor scrubber gets mixed in with the remorse mothers often feel over not spending enough time with their children and not being patient with them. What this does is obscure how really destructive the obedient-child syndrome can be and why it must be exorcised. It stands to reason that if we reflexively respond as obedient children to our husbands and the rest of society, we are bound to respond as children to our own children—that is, resentfully and impatiently. Is it not natural when we are not allowed by ourselves and others to be adults that we relate to our children less maturely? If this strikes a chord of recognition, for heaven's sake, don't blame yourself for not being totally mature. It is not reasonable for this male-dominated society to treat us like children, encouraging us to behave or respond as children and then expect that we will always be mature and wise mothers. Although housework is a real pain, the real issue here is less who does it than *why,* and if the culture expects mothers to be adult, it had better regard us as such.

Unfortunately, that treatment won't be given as a gift, so individually each of us must initiate it by treating ourselves as first-class adult members of society. When we no longer feel we must be "good little girls" and prove ourselves in superficially good behavior that will assure us of receiving approval from everyone, then we can be grown-up mothers to our children. A grown-up mother is one who can put the priorities in order: she and the family come first, high marks for her housekeeping expertise don't even make it to the list. Yes, the housework needs to be done, but not necessarily by a mother who is already holding down a full-time job.

When it comes to spending time with the children, some fathers who don't spend much of it that way may feel they are missing something, but it is doubtful that they feel *guilty* about it, as mothers often do. Again, I think a whale of a lot of energy can be saved if a woman can accept that some things are more important to her than they may be to her husband, and can stop (if that's what she's doing) trying to psychically implant ovaries in a reluctant male. It is more useful to focus on the sorts of things that make her feel guilty about her children and employ some rather simple practices that can make both her and the children feel better. Here are just a few helpful suggestions— some of which apply equally for mothers who stay home—that can get you started thinking about what else might work for you:

- First, remember that your working does not damage your children. Studies have proved that—tell yourself that every day and stop worrying about it. It makes you feel guilty to dwell on that, and guilt diminishes your effectiveness.

- Making the transition from office to home is difficult. A mother can be physically present but actually absent because she's left her mind at the office. Children sense this and often, I think, respond to it with bratty behavior designed to get attention, which, of course, leads to more tension. Take a few minutes at the end of the workday to psyche yourself up for meeting with your children. Sometimes it helps to write down what is preoccupying you before you leave work and tell yourself that you'll forget it temporarily and look at it later in the evening when the children are in bed. Writing things down can get them out of your system temporarily.

- If you can give your child (or each of your children) a few minutes of undivided attention at the end of your workday, quite likely you will find that five or ten minutes will be enough until there's a question or a need of some kind. The child will *take* the time in any case—a piece at a time possibly over a couple of hours. Usually children don't have that much to share with their parents, so if you give them what little they need for their forums, they feel that you care and are interested. And they go off and do something else, and you feel better. And, of course, father should do this, too.

- When your child wants to ask a question, tell you something, or show you something, and you are too busy, try this: tell him or her that you can't (whatever) at this time, but that in fifteen minutes, or when you finish writing this paragraph, reading this page, or chopping up this onion, you will. And then do it. This avoids his or her feeling rejected and your feeling guilty at having said, "I'm too busy," or "Don't bother me now."

- If you feel you don't spend enough time with your child or children, block out some each week on your calendar—as you would a social engagement, an evening meeting, or some other appointment. My kids and I regularly make appointments with each other at the beginning of the week. They love it.

With younger children, you can spend a certain amount of time (say ten or fifteen minutes) several times a week, working a puzzle with big pieces that only takes so long—or playing a game or reading a short story. You don't have to spend whole hours at a time, and if you work this into your schedule or routine, you make the time for it and don't wind up in the position of having your child constantly begging you to play or read to him—which may result in your not doing so and feeling bad, or doing it and feeling resentful and bored.

For older children, here's a nice thing a single mother I know used to do. Each week, she took her three boys out to dinner, and each week the children took turns picking the restaurant and making the reservations. This strikes me as a nice thing for families, including father, to do. And, of course, you can take older children to movies, plays, and concerts that you would like to attend—accomplishing spending time with your children while taking time off for yourself.

- When you or your husband are preparing dinner, get the kids to set the table—mine were about five years old before this suggestion made any sense.

- When you have very young children who go to bed quite early, save any chores you may have for after they are in bed. Keep the time with them as much family time as possible.

- Get older children to help you with some of the chores, such as loading up the dishwasher or washing dishes (you've already made arrangements for cleaning the house, right?).

- Children really do enjoy watching television with their parents. Pick out some shows you can enjoy watching together and then watch them.

- Don't force yourself to do things with your children that you detest doing. Instead, look for those activities that you find enjoyable and include your children in them. I don't, for example, like tennis, so the kids will have to play with someone else. I *do*, however, like to swim and play Frisbee and work jigsaw puzzles, and a number of other things, so those things we do together.

Be Good to Yourself

Now, then, remember that during the discussion of housework, I suggested taking *two days* off from work. Now we come to the second day. After spending the first revamping your routine and thinking of ways to make your relationship with the family a more rewarding one, the second day should be spent doing something exclusively for yourself: resting, reading, shopping, or any other relaxing pleasure you never seem to have time for. All mothers, whether they work or not, need a day off now and then, apart from weekends and holidays that are spent with the family. It is usually guilt that holds them back from leaving children with a sitter for the sole purpose of having some time for themselves. This is especially so for the working mother who may fear that she doesn't give her children enough of her time, and hence any days off should be spent with them. However, mothers must get into the habit of giving their needs a high priority—by doing so, the time they spend with their children is more likely to be given freely and not with resentment. So, if you can't be good to yourself *for* yourself, do it for your kids.

9

The Joy of
Housewifery

If you are a housewife and a young mommy and are regularly exposed to the media while trying to relieve the boredom of folding laundry by watching daytime TV shows, you can get some pretty funny ideas about housework. Subliminally, if not actually, you can get the idea that housework is fun and easy— for example, that scrubbing the kitchen floor only takes as long as a sixty-second commercial for Spic 'n' Span. And following closely behind that idea is that there's something wrong with you because it isn't as easy as it looks on TV and you don't enjoy it all that much.

How do you feel, for example, when you see that stunning creature wearing a white lace dress smilingly cleaning her carpet and enthusing about the glories of Glory? I feel like a frump. And did you ever notice that when the happy ladies on television do their laundry, all the stuff comes out of the dryer not only stain-free but pressed and folded?

And do you ever get the feeling that female persons who have children and stay at home to take care of them should never aspire to expertise in any area other than the cleaning power of certain advertised products? I know, that's not fair of me. Commercials have come a long way. There is, after all, the one about the hospital volunteer. That's the one that shows a wife dressed up in her candy-striper uniform, with hubby proudly looking on and saying, "Hey, you really like this volunteer work, don't you?" She, proving that where there's life, there's growth, answers, "Sure I do. And besides I learn things." What? What does she learn? "Well, I learn what hospitals use to disinfect their bathrooms."

Frankly, slob that I am, it has never occurred to me that it is necessary to disinfect our bathrooms to meet the standards of a hospital examining board. In my limited thinking, I don't see the need for total sterility, simply because our bathrooms are not open to the general public. I must confess that it has never occurred to me to heed the advice of another commercial—to spray all of our beds each week with Lysol. I have exempted myself from that chore, with comfort in the knowledge—however questionable—that this is, after all, our home, and not a bug-infested hotel in a sleazy part of town.

But however much I am able to avoid being manipulated into believing that I should use a lot of products to do a lot of unnecessary tasks, the media still makes a part of me believe that housework is easy, fun, and enriching. And that just maybe …maybe if I use Glory to clean a rug I'll turn into a beautiful twenty-five-year-old model.

The media-inspired cultural notions of housework would be laughable were it not for the fact that disputes over housework can cause marital strife, resentment, anger, guilt, and loss of self-esteem.

In any case, because of the importance that housework can assume, I have a few suggestions for making the job a bit easier. But first, I must emphasize as strongly as possible that it is not my intention to tell other women that they *should* clean their houses or to engender guilt feelings in those who do not. Nor is my aiming my suggestions at homemakers to be construed as advocacy that all mothers *should* be homemakers, a suggestion that all are, or that only women should do housework.

In fact, I think that when the situation is a traditional one and there are children under the age of five, *both* parents should share as much as possible in the care of the children and the housework. Some might argue that this is only valid when a mother works outside the home, and that when a father works hard outside and his wife stays home, she should be totally responsible for the domestic chores because she has the time. The idea is that *he* is tired from working hard all day and shouldn't have to work when he gets home. These arguments ignore some very important *facts:* the mother who works outside the home may well be exhausted at the end of the day and certainly should not be expected to do everything, but when she and the children are out of the house (or there is a housekeeper–baby-sitter) mother hasn't spent her entire work day cleaning up one mess after another and managing young children; it is often implied, on the other hand, that the mother who stays at home does nothing and hence isn't tired after a long day with the children—she therefore has the energy to continue to load the washing machine, cook the dinner, clean up the kitchen, bathe the children, and read them stories. It is more truthful to say that whether a mother works outside or inside the home, she is tired at the end of the day. Put simply, unless they are very rich, *all* mothers of young children *work*.

However, better than my arguments that it seems unfair for a mother to have to just keep going are the words of a father who once believed, as many people do, that when the family is structured traditionally, the lines are clearly drawn. He changed his tune when he temporarily became a "mother."

"I came to really understand," said Bob Peters, "that no one can do that job without a lot of help—and that means more than doing the dishes and flopping on the couch . . . It's those interruptions at the same time. I once forgot I had a twirl cake in the oven and it exploded on me—just because I was a piddling hundred degrees above what Betty Crocker said I should be . . . then there's the endless task of picking up the same marble so many times one day I swore it had trailed me upstairs."

Peters, a former Stanford All-American football player, snapped when he discovered that his children had smeared "his" freshly washed windows while fighting over which TV show to watch. He said he was completely "pooped out" from the total responsibility of being a "housewife." Since "resigning" from the job, Peters not only agrees that he should share equally with his wife but has also hired a housekeeper to come in two days a week.

Now that attitude and act—and not Tidy Bowl or Lysol—may well change life for the Peters family. The combination of sharing support from a husband and household help can make a startling difference in a mother's life. Thus, I think if it is at all affordable, outside services should be used as often as possible— either a cleaning person or a janitorial service, or anything else that can shave some hours off the drudgery and make the total job less overwhelming. Picking up the toys and cleaning up the daily spills are a lot more bearable when on top of it you don't have to scour showers, strip and wax floors, wash windows, and clean the oven. Just having someone come in *once a month* can make a difference. It's a better bargain than most people think it is.

However, I don't expect to see a major revolution as a result of either my written advocacies or Bob Peters's public confession that housework did him in. Right now, even though more mothers are returning to work, there remain large numbers of them either ensconced in or about to move into the traditional arrangement.

A Common Trap New Homemakers Can Fall Into

Some women tend not to realize when they quit their jobs and settle into housewifery that doing all the work will be different with children on the scene—not the snap it was when there were just two adults. So, the setup for disappointment and failure exists. For example, a friend of mine, who quit her job just before her first baby was due, enthusiastically embraced homemaking after working in an office and making a pass at it only on weekends. During the month before the baby arrived, she kept an impeccable house. After he was born, he slept most of the time, so maintaining that standard wasn't terribly difficult—and she had time to prepare wonderful meals, bake, and sew. She very much enjoyed fussing over the house, embellishing it with handmade touches and bringing in freshly cut flowers regularly. Gradually, her child slept fewer hours, and gradually she had less time to fuss. When the baby started to walk, she had even *less* time because she had to watch him more closely, chase him around the house, and kiss scraped knees. At about this time she became pregnant with her second child. By the time that child was born, my friend's domestic expertise had slipped considerably, even though she spent nearly every waking hour working. Although she understoood why, she felt like a failure. And to make matters worse, her husband had grown accustomed to a well-ordered home and magnificent meals and didn't understand at all why things had changed.

The point is, obviously, don't set standards you won't be able to live up to, thereby setting yourself up as a failure either in your eyes or in your husband's eyes later on. And if you already have, and are working night and day to keep your home looking like a television commercial, start gradually easing off. If you are just getting started as a homemaker, remember that a little dust around the edges may be an investment toward future peace of mind. And you would do well to realize that the first burst of enthusiasm you might feel for domesticity frequently isn't enough to keep the boredom and frustration away when it starts to get old.

I think it's a mistake to have as your goal pleasing or impressing others with your homemaking expertise. Even when those others include only family members, you're still in the trap of conducting yourself on the basis of what other people will think of you. That puts those others in charge of you. It can also lead them to equate love with a clean house, laundered clothes, and good meals, which in turn can lead them to equate periodic disinterest in homemaking with disinterest in them—or lack of love.

Quite possibly there would be fewer arguments about housework in general if whoever was responsible for most of it approached it from a standpoint of pleasing himself or herself. (I know several single people, for example, who are really good housekeepers and good cooks and who like doing these things because it gives *them* pleasure.)

When you try to keep house nicely and cook well to please your husband, I think it gives him a wedge that he can use against you. When it's important to you that he thinks you are a perfect homemaker—and he knows it—it makes you vulnerable to criticism when you fall short of the mark. When he's angry at you for something that has nothing whatever to do with the house, he can punish you by finding a smudge on the windows or something dead and rotting in the refrigerator. If you don't have your worth tied up in such things, then, obviously, that sort of dirty fighting won't work.

Getting Out of the Trap

If you are already caught between reality and your husband's expectation that perfection is always possible because it once existed in your home, there is a way to drive home the point that taking care of active children and a house isn't exactly a lark. One woman in such a position told me that her husband, who really is a kind man, had the annoying habit of thinking that her life at home with the children was a bed of roses, and that it was his hard work that made it that way. Although he sat down in a clean dining room to a nicely prepared meal at the end of each day, he felt that his wife did virtually nothing with her time. He never questioned how it was that he had clean clothes in his closet, that his children's needs were seen to—indeed, he had no idea what they might be—and that his life ran pretty smoothly. And periodically, when it didn't run so smoothly and he came home from work to find his wife yelling at the children and the house in disarray, he'd ask, "What's wrong with you? You had the whole day to yourself—"

"When I'd start to list all of the things I do," she said, "he'd tune me out. Or say something like, 'Yes, yes, you have a hard life—just like a pioneer woman.' Then one day, after he'd laid that on me the night before, I just didn't do anything at all except give the children their meals. When my husband walked through the door that evening—with a client, no less—that place looked like a cyclone had come through: there were toys strewn from one end of the house to the other, the dishes from two meals and numerous snacks were scattered about, the garbage bags and wastebaskets were spilling over, the beds weren't made, his clothes were on the floor where he'd left them the night before, as were the children's. I said, in my calmest voice, 'You often wonder what's wrong with me—why I get frustrated. And you ask what I do all day. Well, *today* I didn't do it.'"

Better yet, not only to provide a husband with some feeling of the actual chores you do all day but to give him some feeling for the whole domestic scene, if possible arrange for him to take over. My friend and neighbor did just that. She called her husband one day at his office and told him she had to go to Los Angeles on emergency family business—her sister was ill and needed her to come and look after the children. She said she would be leaving that afternoon before their children came home from school. When he stammered and stalled about their care, she explained that he would either have to come home or make arrangements. She told him that the list of sitters she regularly used was tacked on the wall near the phone. And, no, she didn't know exactly when she'd be back. Her husband got quite a taste of what it was like not only to be a mother and a homemaker, but also, on those days when he absolutely had to be at the office, what it might be like to be a *working* mother as well.

A few years ago, I went on three separate trips which totaled about four weeks altogether. Since my husband gets a generous vacation from his company every year, we decided that instead of hiring a sitter-housekeeper, which would be expensive, he would take his vacation during those weeks I would be gone. Ever since, when I've told him that I've had it up to here with the kids and the house, he says, "I know, I know," in a tone that tells me he does indeed know precisely what I'm talking about.

At the Other End of the Spectrum

For some women, the lack of enthusiasm, the boredom, and the frustration of trying to maintain a neat home while children undo their work has caused their homemaking to slip so much that they do virtually nothing. An extreme example is a woman I know who seems to feel that her housekeeping chores are some kind of infringement on her activities, which now consist primarily of watching television, gossiping with the neighbors, and talking on the telephone. She takes time out only to change a diaper, put a bandage on a cut, make sandwiches for lunch, and throw something together and call it dinner. She is a good and loving mother, but an overworked housekeeper, or a housekeeper at all, she isn't—not by any stretch of the imagination.

When her husband comes home from work he adds to the mess by hanging his coat on a doorknob, letting his shoes drop where they may, flinging his dirty socks across the room, and then slumping into a chair with a beer and his newspaper, the remains of which will be scattered around by the time he sits down to dinner. He yells at his wife that the house is a filthy mess and asks her what the hell she does all day. She responds by telling him that he's a pig and no one can keep a clean house with him tossing junk all over the room. He counters by saying that the place is such a wreck that it doesn't matter what he does and that he has no incentive to act any differently.

She tells *me* she's bored, her husband expects too much, doesn't appreciate her, and is the most unreasonable bastard on the face of the earth. She complains that he never pays her a compliment but instead criticizes her constantly. And then she laments, "Even though I know he's wrong to pick on me I feel guilty."

Of course she feels guilty. She made a bargain with this man that held that he would support her and the children and she would maintain the home. Whether it is a sexist bargain or not, and whether she feels that he's fortunate because he can go out every day into the exciting world of commerce while she's stuck at home with the kids, she *knows* that she is not, in any appreciable way, keeping her part of the deal and she feels guilty about it. How could she not? Her husband works fifty hours a week to support the family, and although a mother is always on call, I would estimate that this particular mother's actual work time turns out to be about ten hours a week. The woman behaves as if she were permanently on vacation. Just as is the case with misbehaving children, I think that most adults feel guilty not only when what they are doing is wrong, but when they are allowed to get away with it. This woman's guilt problems are, to me, ones that could be avoided with even minimal effort. Much of her problem could be alleviated if she would simply stay off the phone or turn off the television set long enough to do a few of the simpler chores.

I guess I have to say that heavy addiction to television during the day has just got to be either a cause or symptom of self-hate. Either you hate yourself for it, or it's a way of telling yourself that you can't do anything else. However much one would enjoy it (which I question), it isn't living, and doing only that cannot contribute much to feeling good about yourself. If kicking the habit cold turkey is too formidable a task, then how about, if you are hooked, having some television-watching chores, like:

- Ironing
- Mending
- Folding laundry
- Filing your fingernails
- Flossing your teeth
- Cleaning out boxes of junk
- Putting photo albums in shape
- Straightening up the room where the TV sits
- Hand crafts of any kind

How to Make Housework More Bearable

The last thing in the world I would tell *anyone* is that house-work is *fun*. But with that said, I must admit that there are ways that you can make it at least bearable. And a secret I'll share with you is that the women I know who are the most successful in getting their important chores accomplished and keeping their homes looking nice, truly *hate* housework. These women hate it so much that they have as a goal getting it over with as quickly as possible so they don't have to think about it in addition to doing it.

I cannot prescribe for everyone, and I have certainly had my share of monkey wrenches thrown into my machinery, but for what it may be worth to you, my own routine has worked well for me for years. Naturally, there have been variations, depend-ing on the ages of the children and whether or not I had an outside job or was engaged, as I am right now, in a very engross-ing writing project. But some parts of it might work out well for you or perhaps can be adapted to your routine. Before offering my routine, however, I should say that the two things that have made my housekeeping life the easiest are (1) the setting of priorities, and (2) having as a top priority keeping the house *neat*—as neat as is possible when people live in a place. You can't really clean the house if there's stuff strewn all over the place, and nobody ever has been injured by a dirty window, but legs and arms have been broken from tripping over stuff sitting out in the middle of the floor. Anyway, this is approximately the routine I follow:

- Get up before anyone else. Sleeping later than the rest of the family by even fifteen minutes can set you back for hours. Allow enough time for a quiet cup of coffee or tea to collect your morning wits.

- If you have a dishwasher and you haven't unloaded the dinner dishes the night before, do it after the coffee.
- If you have babies or young children who go through lots of clothes, throw clothes into the washer.
- Get as much of the breakfast ready as possible before the rest of the family gets up.
- Empty any garbage, ashtrays, etc.
- As soon as everyone is up, fed, and essentially set for the day, make the beds.
- Clear away the breakfast dishes and get rid of the garbage.

This was, and for the most part still is, my early morning schedule. And the reason I devote so much time and space to dishes, making beds, and emptying the garbage is that I find unmade beds, dishes in the sink, and garbage spilling all over the place depressing. And these are chores that are easily dispensed with, so why let them hang around to weigh on your mind. Anyway, I continue this way:

- If my feet stick to the kitchen floor, I mop it.
- As soon as everyone is relatively squared away, I make a list of everything I have to do (more accurately, I update my ongoing list). (Marabel Morgan did not, by the way, invent the making of lists. Nor is her method the last word—the last word is Alan Laekin who wrote *How to Get Control of Your Time and Your Life,* a book I recommend. My list-making started years ago when I was a secretary to a tyrant who wanted everything done last month. To keep it all straight, I would assign everything a priority. That was when I learned that some things that fall very low on the priority list really don't need to be done—they are frills that are frequently mistakenly seen as necessities.)

- Then I start working on the items on my list, taking one thing at a time and staying with it until it is finished. When my children were quite young, I took full advantage of nap times and playpens—but I made it a policy to *always* give in to an urge to cuddle a child.

- At some point, I learned to plan for crisis—to leave my schedule loose enough to allow for those things that cannot be scheduled, such as sick children, cut knees, toddlers needing to crawl up on laps (and later ten-year-olds who need a sympathetic ear and a hug), stopped-up toilets, spilled food and drink, and all of the sorts of things that can lay to rest the best-made plans. You need not cower in a state of paranoia, but it is wise to know that anything can happen.

- Early in the day, sometimes while preparing lunch, I start putting together pieces of dinner so that it isn't all left for the hazardous dinner hour. And this is a good place to recommend the many wonderful cookbooks—from Betty Crocker to haute cuisine—that contain recipes for good make-ahead dinners.

- Errands. First, make a list. Don't even think about actually running an errand without a list. Next, look at the list and see how many of your errands can be accomplished by letting your fingers do the walking, and then call and order for delivery, or make inquiries, to trim your errand-running list. Then, plan to run all of your errands on the same day—I usually run them once a week. When the children were younger, I hired someone to look after them while I did this. I recommend it.

Over the years I have developed a basic philosophy about housework. At one time I tried to maintain an absolutely perfect home. I felt then that, in addition to a routine straightening of the house every day, it was *vital* that it receive a thorough cleaning once a week (that included such things as spot-cleaning the living room carpet and vacuuming the drapery). At some point I realized that people, even husbands who are perfectionists, don't really notice or comment if you have done a pristine and splendid job, but surely do if you haven't. And when it is all mostly perfect, any flaws, no matter how small, stand out like sore thumbs. For example, when I would strip and wax the black-and-white checkerboard floor in our foyer and dining room, if there were two toys sitting on it when my husband came home from work he would notice the toys but not the back-breaking wax job I'd done. There are few strokes and few breaks in the routine for the perfect housekeeper, and we all need some of both.

And I have to be honest about how I feel about all of the time I spent scrubbing and polishing. I'd give anything if I could turn back the clock. When I think about how impatient I would become with the children because I *absolutely had to* spit and polish a floor or a window, I feel remorse at valuing something so superficial over a child's self-esteem. I often wonder, too, if I might not have enjoyed spending time with the children more if I didn't have the sense, when I *was* enjoying them, that I should be cleaning something or other in the house. The black-and-white floor has become a symbol to me. It's not even mine—or ours, I should say (although I always felt a certain ownership because of the work)—anymore. We sold the house and moved into another—more beautiful and whose tile and wood floors are care-free—and those black-and-white floors are no better or worse for all the polishing. They are static—about the same as ever. My children, however, are not—their baby years are gone. The mother I am today wouldn't waste herself keeping the place looking like *House Beautiful*. House Relatively Neat is good enough—as I said, it's a question of priorities.

I think it's appropriate to point out that during a long drought I was fully vindicated for my relaxed attitude. The water shortage in California taught many of us that there is such a thing as too clean. It is amazing how well we natives adapted to wearing garments more than once, not changing our sheets every week, using our towels for longer than usual, living with opaque windows, driving dirty cars, and not nagging our children to take showers or baths every day. For the sake of your sanity, and in the interest of conserving water, you may want to consider resisting the insistence of television commericals that would have you strive to be cleaner than clean. However, at the same time, I heartily recommend such obvious time-savers as permanent-press clothes and absolutely anything else that makes your job easier. A word of caution on convenience items: don't buy anything that promises to make your work load easier but introduces a new job you hadn't thought of; for example, carpet deodorizers that you spray on and vacuum up—unless, of course, the place smells like a sty.

How about Getting the Kids to Help?

Every time the subject of housework comes up, someone says something like, "Well, children can and should help." While this is true, whoever says it doesn't mention that (a) even when they are perfectly capable of helping—say around five or so—they are still making messes, and (b) that getting the kids to help requires a rather large effort on the part of the parents. The statement, without these qualifiers, has a way of creating feelings of inadequacy in parents who thus far haven't been about to whip everyone into shape. And also, at least for several years, giving the children responsibility for household chores is mostly something that parents do not for themselves but for the chil-

dren—to teach independence. Yes, some children want to help.
But other children need to be nagged, coerced, supervised, and
cleaned up after—after they do the job—well into the teen years.
I feel that to believe otherwise is just another setup for failure
and something that can set the stage for fireworks between
parents and children.

Lisa and Adam *do* help around the house and they *do* have
specific chores. But a lot of *my* time and *my* energy went into
teaching them how to do certain things, while stifling the impulse to do it myself and get it over with so I could spend the
"teaching time" doing something else that needed to be done or
that I wanted to do. Let's not oversimplify this notion of children
helping. It takes time, energy, and patience. And any parent
who is presently overwhelmed is not emotionally geared to it.

And Now a Word about Children's Rooms

After listening to many mothers talk, and knowing my own
feelings and experiences, I see children's rooms as a great source
of maternal guilt. If the children don't keep their rooms neat,
we see that as a result of our having trained them inadequately.
On the other hand, we feel that perhaps we should keep their
rooms neat and that when we don't, we are being lousy, neglectful mothers. Furthermore, this is the subject of many a heated
argument in many homes. Some fathers feel that if the children's rooms look like boars' nests it's the fault of the mother—
that other children in other families are different. Mothers nag
children, children become hostile, wars are waged. As one mother
told me, "It hit me one day that I was going to totally destroy
my relationship with my daughter if I didn't just close the door
to her room and forget it was part of this house."

Making matters worse for all of us is that the children's rooms
we see on television and in the magazines are perfect and

believable—we see them so often that they seem more normal to us than the ones that we know to be usual—in our own homes. The media bedrooms give us dreams that we can emulate them. If we clean our children's rooms and then watch them deteriorate before our very eyes in a matter of minutes we feel resentful. We feel even more resentful if we have spent money and elbow grease decorating them and this happens. When my own children were ready to come out of the nursery and have real bedrooms of their own, I did just that very thing. Their bedrooms were lovely for two whole weeks after I painted, made curtains, and bought beautiful bedspreads and accessories. Since then, I've come up with some rules I try to live by:

- Purchase the bottom-of-the-line carpeting for a child's room. Shag rugs are absolutely out—they are unsafe for young children because dangerous objects get hidden in them, and unaesthetic for older children's rooms because chewing gum and food stick their yarns together. Linoleum is ideal unless a child's room has a slab foor, in which case you'll want to use cheap *(cheap, cheap)* carpeting so the room's occupant won't break a leg falling out of bed.

- Furniture should be safe, easy to clean, and nothing you cherish. Avoid sharp corners, poisonous paints, or unstable pieces of furniture that children can pull over on themselves.

- From about age three on, try to encourage neatness. You can show a child how to make a bed and encourage him or her to pick up their toys and clothes, but don't expect a great deal— uncomplicated clothes hampers, by the way, are much better than those "darling" little hanging bags that hold about three socks. It's good to remember that when you tell even a ten-year-old to clean up his or her room, he or she views that in the same way as you might view someone telling you to build a house.

- If the room is safe enough for a child to be in unsupervised, or if the child is old enough, go in only to pick up and deliver the laundry, change the sheets, and collect any food that may be rotting somewhere.
- And when you go in, psyche yourself out to fully expect the room to look like a scene from *Earthquake*. At this moment, try to remember that some people—even some child-guidance specialists—believe that neat children may be unbalanced.
- Avoid hysteria.

Childproofing Can Preserve Your Mental Health

Because I am a parent and because I write about parenthood, I either have read or skimmed just about every popular child-related book ever published. And the one thing that *all* experts agree on is that the wise mother childproofs her house. But none that I know of tells you precisely how to do it. Because there are numerous things a mother can do to prevent a variety of disasters guaranteed to drive her crazy, I have some suggestions. You may have already won blue ribbons in childproofing or your children may be old enough so that it is not needed. But in the event that it can be helpful and because I think these rules should appear all together somewhere, here are mine for the safety of the children and the sanity of the mother:

- Cover all electrical outlets not in use with blanks. You can buy them at any hardware or variety store.
- And speaking of electricity, never, never leave an extension cord not in use plugged in—children put *everything* into their mouths. (When he was eleven, my son put a tack in his mouth—while he was *talking* to me no less.) This is just one of the many things that can kill or maim.

- And speaking now of cords, try to secure those that are attached to lamps and small appliances so that children cannot use them to pull such items over on themselves. Also stay alert to cords being objects that young children have been known to chew on.

- Store all poisons, cleaning solvents, and medicines in locked cabinets. It probably isn't practical to store your dishwashing detergent that way, but do keep it and *all* cleaning supplies up high and out of the reach of children and maintain an awareness that these things are lethal.

- Store small objects, such as pins, buttons, marbles, paper clips, anything sharp, and so forth, safely out of reach.

- All matches and cigarette lighters should be put up high and any furniture or accessories that can be dangerous should either be childproofed or removed.

- Everyone knows that decals should be placed at eye level on plate-glass doors and windows that are like doors that someone might accidentally walk through or bounce off.

- Put gates at the top of all stairs (you may want to put them at the bottom too) and in the doorways of all rooms that pose a threat to your child or vice versa.

- Fancy new houses often have small bolts placed high at the top of all doors, but inexpensive hook-and-eyes (the ones you screw into the wood) work well for keeping children out of rooms and closets. Put them high on bathroom doors, too.

- Because anyone who has ever had the experience of having a child lock himself into the bathroom knows that terrible things can happen, they would be apt to tell you that children under five years of age should never be left alone in the bathroom, because, obviously, there are razor blades, medicines, hot water, electrical doodads, and all sorts of things that are both fascinating and dangerous. And even if the room is fully childproofed (which is doubtful), there's always the toilet that can be put out of commission from having blocks or toys flushed down it. And this is as good a place as any to mention that a child under five should *never* be left alone in the tub. It isn't just that the child might drown, but he or she might also get scalded turning on the hot water.

- But, you can have your plumber set the thermostat on your water heater at a lower temperature to prevent scalding water from coming through the pipes.

- In the kitchen (and elsewhere), store all breakable items in high cupboards and use the lower ones for canned goods, packaged foods, pots and pans—all things that children like and can play with safely. If you want to keep children out of cupboards altogether and if you have handles instead of knobs on the doors and drawers, you can use rubber vine "tie-backs" to keep your cupboards "locked" (they are inexpensive and most hardware stores carry them) and insert a yardstick straight down through the handles in a row of drawers.

- I think we all know that one should turn pot handles to the back of the stove, use the back burners to cook on, and never leave the kitchen in the first place if it contains small children and cooking food—in fact, it's not a good idea to leave small children running around alone in the kitchen in any case.

- Dr. Spock advises parents to pack books tight into bookshelves so that children can't pull them out and tear them to shreds. This really works only if the bookshelves are attached to the wall or are sturdy and weighted well at the bottom, because a strong, determined child can pull the whole thing over on himself.

- If you have your milk delivered to your home, request that it come in cartons and not in bottles—those bottles that you leave out to be picked up can be an attractive and extremely dangerous nuisance.

- I like screen doors although I actually hate the way they look. But they come in handy on front and back entrances when you are answering the door and trying to keep children and animals inside. If you have a porch that a child might fall off, a latched screen door is helpful.

- Speaking of exterior doors, a friend told me that putting on spring-type door returns (so that you won't have to scream at older children a thousand times a day to, "SHUT THE DOOR!") is a bad idea because a child can lose a finger in one (she knew of one child who did).

- Don't store temptations such as cookies in a cupboard over the stove. Even if your children are older, say nine or ten, should you leave the room for a moment when the pots are boiling, a quick reach for a cookie can set a sleeve on fire.

- Hang your paper towels high and not over the stove or over a kitchen counter. You will prevent accidents and save a fortune.

- New and expectant mothers should be advised that water softeners can be dangerous—soft water makes for slippery babies at bath time.

- Make a list of all emergency numbers and tape it to the wall near the phone. Put 911 at the top of the list, so that if anything happens that flusters you too much to call your doctor, you can call that number.

- My mother told me that when I was three years old I pulled an entire Christmas tree over on me—which is why we don't have any of those wonderful old-fashioned decorations anymore. I have seen my children do nearly the same thing. Be very aware of the passion a young child has for the Christmas tree and watch closely. Or you can do as some friends of ours did—they put the Christmas tree in the playpen.

- I came closer than I can bear to think about to losing my eight-year-old son to an empty refrigerator on the back porch. It was not abandoned but it was empty and the shelves had been removed. Don't have empty refrigerators, freezers, or any similar temptation around the place. It takes only one encounter for them to visit you with the worst disaster a mother can know.

10

How to Turn Your Husband into Your Own Best Friend

When we were married we were so in love and couldn't imagine something so rare and so deep would ever change. With the birth of the first child, this of course changed. I believe the greatest reason I resent my children is for the damage they did to a beautiful relationship. I feel that I've been robbed and cheated and will never recapture that which I treasured so much. Anyway, that is reality, and we must go on.

Ray's wife

So, you've put the daisy in the toilet to surprise your husband, as Lois Bird, author of *How to Turn Your Husband into Your Lover,* advises. And you've met him at the door wearing a Saran Wrap, as *Total Woman* Marabel Morgan might suggest—and possibly dashed home from work to set the stage for romance with drinks and candlelight. He walks through the door and finds his usually tired wife weaving about like a siren while hungry children whine in the background. And all that has happened is that he now *believes* you when you say the kids are driving you crazy. Who knows? Getting him to worry that you are now certifiable may well get you the support you need. But a modest suggestion I have, based on the assumption that a mother needs all the friends she can get and as little marital strife as possible, is that you try turning your husband into your best friend.

One of the greatest barriers to building a friendship with a spouse is also one of the fundamental causes of problems in a marital relationship—most of us expect too much from marriage *and each other.* Richard B. Austin, Jr., author of *How to Make It with Another Person,* says, for example, that "underlying the fiction that 'marriage will make me happy,' is the idea that marriage, by some magic, will solve all our personal problems and meet all our needs. This fiction places an oppressive burden on one's mate and robs the relationship—and its participants—of potential joy.

"Everyone," he continues, "has psychological needs for recognition, approval, security, belonging, and growth—needs which may be partially met in marriage. But while husbands and wives may contribute to their partners' sense of well-being, no one has the power to create happiness for another."[1]

I agree. But with some reservations. The other side of that idea is that no one can make you unhappy unless you allow them to. Popular thought, based on some new therapies and theories and some old Easten diciplines, adheres rather strictly to the idea that you and you alone are responsible for the way you feel. When you can get to the point where you believe this, it can be a comforting and reinforcing idea. However, it does give some people license to run roughshod over others, with no concern for whether their acts or words have the potential to hurt ("It's not my fault that you're upset because I just called you an ugly fat cow—after all, according to Dr. So-and-So, my behavior belongs to me and cannot upset you unless you allow it to.").

The responses of human beings are often learned, of course, but they are also reflexive. Reading that you feel the way you do because you allow it is, in my opinion, another way of being told how you *should* feel. That is, if there is a choice in the matter and you sincerely do not wish to feel bad, then you should make yourself feel otherwise. When popular guides on relationships disseminate this concept, there is an assumption, first, that there are blueprints for feelings; next, that those going through trauma have read and accepted them, and, finally, that at a given moment, you can push the appropriate emotional button and respond to a cutting remark as a lab animal might.

I become even less certain that one is the author of all of his or her emotions when I apply this theory to my own life. I know, for example, that when my husband is upset with me about something, or has said something hurtful to me, no matter how little responsibility I am willing to assume for his actions, I feel pain. If I tell myself I have a choice in how I feel, it doesn't help because feelings are feelings. I do not believe, based on my experiences, that I can engineer my feelings.

Thus, I *do* believe that while we may not have the power to make someone else happy, we do have the power to make other people feel utterly miserable—to hurt, enrage, and arouse guilt feelings, and even drive another person crazy. To dismiss this power with the simplistic jargon of a current fad is a denial that responsibility goes along with a commitment to another person. You may ultimately be able to come to some sort of terms with the idea that you bear a certain amount of responsibility for your feelings and reactions, but abdication of your responsibility for the feelings of another is antithetical to a caring relationship.

One of the ways in which married people can hurt one another starts out with those high expectations that Richard Austin and other experts speak of. Most of us begin our marriages expecting far more of our spouses than we *ourselves* are either capable of or willing to deliver. We demand undying love and devotion and the total acceptance of *our* flaws, while nearly insisting that our spouses be flawless. Then, after being repeatedly disappointed that our marriages and the people we chose as our partners fall short of the ideal we have set, some of us continue to expect that which our spouses have demonstrated they cannot give—and when we do not receive, we become resentful. Or, at some point, we decide to forcefully make them over into our images of what we think they should be. *I can think of no greater insult nor more resounding rejection, either to give or receive, than this sort of nonacceptance.*

Thus, it would seem that an important step to take if you want to turn a marriage into a friendship is acceptance. Acceptance, first, of the relationship itself as a limited partnership and not some sort of magical union that will meet all our needs, and, next, acceptance of the people we are married to—with all of their human imperfections. I'm not suggesting, of course, that cruelty, unfairness, or objectionable behavior be included in this acceptance. A person *can* change his *behavior,* and if you find it offensive, it's fair to say so. However, he can't change what he *is.* If, for example, you are married to a quiet man, don't expect that he can be manipulated into being the life of the party. If he's not interested in everything you are interested in, doesn't have the same tastes as you have, or doesn't hold the same philosophies that you do, no amount of demanding will change that. He can't change how he feels, either, just because you might want him to. If he's not cut out to be a high-powered, money-making businessman, or more or less athletic than he is, there is nothing you can do to make him otherwise. So, don't make your disappointment over what he fundamentally is (which may be an unfair appraisal of him) obvious by demanding that he be something else. You have no right to insist on it. You will only hurt him very deeply. It works both ways, of course, and if *either* or *both* of you behave this way, the guilty parties must stop it or the marriage will never work. Acceptance of reality and each other, in my opinion, is fundamental to a relationship of any substance.

When Lovers Are Only Friends

At some point, a problem that really isn't a problem at all is likely to crop up in marriage. I think we all know that the relationship that remains passionate or romantic from the beginning to the tenth year is rare. As we settle into marriage we accept that ardor comes in waves, not an unending torrent. But what some people don't seem to realize, according to psychiatrist Dr. David Viscott, is that there are times in the best of marriages when one partner or the other (or both of them at the same time) falls out of love. Viscott advises people to recognize this as a *normal* occurrence and realize that the love *will come back*.[2]

I wonder how many people are aware of this. I wonder how many times it has happened that a husband or wife has temporarily fallen out of love with his or her partner, and the other person, sensing the absence of this all-important feeling, has been hurt and felt deep enough resentment so that it has damaged the relationship.

Or, how many times, during such a period, one partner has fallen out of love with his or her spouse and "fallen *in* love" with someone else and had an affair—and then fallen back in love at some point with his or her partner only to find that there was no forgiveness for an infidelity?

I am sure it often would turn out differently if the "injured party" had some awareness that people do fall out of love temporarily, and when this happens they are especially vulnerable to infatuation. I'm not for a moment discounting the pain that one might feel when he or she is confronted with what appears to be evidence of no longer being loved—but I do think that a fuller than traditional understanding of what may be occurring might lessen the pain and the fears.

Finally, I wonder how many couples who genuinely may have the capacity to love each other for life have simultaneously hit these normal lows that Viscott describes at the same time that other conflicts might be taking place—and then concluded that it was time to end the marriage, only to regret it later when feelings of love returned.

How different it might be for these hypothetical couples if they possessed some awareness of Dr. Viscott's observations. How different it might be if they were able to float through these periods knowing that "even if you can't be lovers all the time, you still can be friends." How different it could be for all of us if we could grasp the fact that it is normal for our love to go through cycles and vary in intensity, instead of expecting the impossible romantic dream to be a constant. The problem that really doesn't exist then might be "solved," and other problems prevented by insuring that, in addition to love, we have a firm base of friendship to fall back on when love temporarily takes a leave of absence.

And then there are times when love doesn't take a leave of absence, but we conclude that it may have on the basis of "evidence" that it isn't as vibrant at the moment as it once was. Even though we may have warm and positive feelings toward a person we love, when those feelings don't manifest themselves in passionate sexual desire we may worry that we are no longer in love. Similarly, when the warm feelings directed toward *us* are expressed only in affection, we may see that as evidence that our partners are no longer in love with *us*. Then we move on to feeling undesirable, which hurts our vanity, and rejected, which hurts our feelings.

Society conspires today to make us feel sexually fearful and performance-oriented. Just about any day of the week you can pick up a newspaper or a magazine and find a test or read an article that tells you that you are inadequate, your partner is, both of you are, or that you or he are doing something to turn each other off. And sometimes you can read into that a sense that your marriage is in serious trouble.

I have heard men say that they felt they weren't good lovers and women say that they felt there was something wrong with them. When I've asked what made them feel that way, the answer was always prefaced with, "Well, I was reading that . . ."

When we brought sex out of the closet and pushed it straight into the spotlight, we made sex the star of the show, elevating it to *the* most important element in any loving relationship. By blueprinting how it should work for maximum performance and instituting comparative scoring, we robbed individual intimate experience of uniqueness, while killing spontaneity by mechanizing it.

There are lots of reasons why people in love are not always eager to make love: fatigue, worry, preoccupation, other priorities at the moment are just a few. Worrying about why you or your partner may show disinterest from time to time creates a pressure that need not exist, to say nothing of pointless doubts and fears about the relationship. But then, how many times have we heard that when a marriage is in trouble the first thing to go is sex? I've heard it hundreds of times, and yet even Masters and Johnson will say it isn't necessarily so. Frequency and technique, in my opinion, have absolutely nothing to do with love.

With all the media hype about sex, we need to remind ourselves that this is but a part of our marital lives together and that all of us are different and subject to all manner of different environmental forces. Anyway, love is not a three-letter word.

The Impact of Children on Marriage

Unfortunately, the time when love and friendship are most likely to take a vacation together from marriage is the time when the presence of both is the most important. As early as 1957, E. E. LeMasters, reporting in *Marriage and Family Living,* wrote that extensive or severe home crisis situations occurred following the birth of a child in 83 percent of the cases he studied.[3] Arthur P. Jacoby, writing in the *Journal of Marriage and the Family,* goes a bit further and says that 87 percent of new parents were disturbed rather than pleased with the changed family situation.[4] Dr. Harold Feldman, a professor in the Department of Human Development and Family Studies at Cornell University, puts it more simply: "When a couple become parents the marital satisfaction declines."[5]

And Richard B. Austin, Jr., sums up, in more human and specific terms, what the majority of us already know because of our own realities: "Two people in love often find their own world shattered by cries in the night, dirty diapers, and general confinement to the home. Privacy is largely eliminated by young children. A 'turned-on' sex life, which demands spontaneity and time, may be dimmed by knocks on the closed door or by the usual noises that children make." He also points out, "Children in our modern society are expensive . . . the fact that money problems often contribute heavily to marital discord means that children may prove to be the straw that breaks the back of a marriage . . ."[6]

The paradox, obviously, is that most of the time we think children not only will make us happy but will also solidify our marriages, and when instead they create strains in a relation-

ship, we are disappointed and resentful toward them and, perhaps irrationally, toward our spouses. Worse yet, marital problems can so affect our emotions that we have more difficulty
than usual in dealing with our children, which, coming full
vicious cycle, puts more strain on the marriage.

According to most experts, children have the greatest negative impact on marriage when they first arrive because the
change in the life-style is more dramatically felt at that time.
Many mothers I've talked to believe that the first five years
generally are very difficult ones because children need continual care then, which makes being a wife more difficult. They
also feel that when the children get into mischief husbands tend
to be critical of the mothers, which creates a lot of friction: "Why
do you let him do these things—*you're* the adult?" "You just try
to keep up with him—you just don't even *want* to understand."
It is when the children start "doing these things" that couples
may discover that their attitudes about discipline are at the
opposite ends of the pole—one may be strict, the other permissive, which leads them to blame each other, criticize each other,
and in the case of the permissive parent, protect the child from
the stricter one, who then becomes angry at having his or her
authority undermined.

The bad news is that even when the children begin to be more
civilized and start school, the situation doesn't get much better.
According to sociologist Jessie Bernard, children from six to
fourteen "seem to have an especially distressing effect on marriage." The source of the trouble, again, is conflicting child-
rearing ideas *and blame-fixing*. Also, in a traditional marriage
this generally is a period when a man is devoting most of his
energies to his career, so all the pressures fall more heavily on
a wife.[7] I'm inclined to think that when *both* are working to
establish themselves in their careers, this still holds true—that

if one career is to suffer because of the children, I'll bet hers is the one to be affected, which doesn't exactly make for loving feelings.

The teen years are particularly hard on a marriage, and the situation doesn't seem to improve until the children leave home. Some researchers report that this is a time—when the children leave home—that parents who have stayed together for the sake of the children get the divorces they say they've always wanted; on the other hand, it can be a time when couples once again find each other. Happily, I have known more of the latter than the former.

The best advice I can give you comes from these parents—those who have made it through and come out on top with good marriages. They all say that what saved it for them was having realistic expectations of each other, respect, understanding, and compassion, and a keen awareness that the problems they were having with each other existed not because of a lack of love for each other but because of the problems that are universally part of raising a family.

Thus, a genuine awareness that children can play havoc in a marriage helps, along with remembering back to what it was like before the children came along and recalling the feelings you had for one another. They are probably still there but can get buried under the weight of the day-to-day coping with parenthood. While recognizing that it will never be quite the same again—and that change in a relationship is inevitable in any case—parents at least ought to stop blaming each other if their child-battered marriage is not in the best of condition. While a husband may be held accountable because he doesn't understand—or at least try to understand—what a mother might be feeling, he shouldn't be held responsible for all of a wife's unhappiness and all marital ills.

Virtually everyone who advises on marriage enhancement tells couples they should have time away from their children; as regularly as possible, they should arrange for child care and go out to dinner or a movie or some other mutual entertainment. Redundantly, I second that. But I would like to add that the woman who silently suffers from not having a break in the routine and finally petulantly accuses, "You never take me anywhere," gets no sympathy from me. Understanding yes, sympathy no. I really *do* understand the perverse pleasure of self-pity and making hubby out to be a thoughtless bastard. But because it can be a source of genuine misery and doesn't get you anywhere beyond stuck in the house, I'm not sympathetic. Sure, it would be nice if *he* thought of it and made the arrangements. But when *he* doesn't, then *you've* got to. Instead of moaning about it and holding out for lightning to strike and turn him into instantly thoughtful, call a sitter and take *him* out for an evening once in a while. Let him know what you want and why before it gets to be such a bone of contention that neither of you gets anything out of it.

Lunch is just as good as an evening out for some couples. In fact, some people—my husband is one of them—feel that it's even better because people are mellower and less tired at lunchtime, and it is a more unusual treat. It's up to you to make sure that time alone together happens.

Some of His and Her Complaints

Many women—even some who work full time—tell me that when they become frustrated or overwhelmed with domestic chores their husbands become *offended*—offended that they are not totally fulfilled by their homemaking roles, taking it personally when their wives don't love scrubbing johns and wiping noses. How absurd! And irritating. But, then, fathers haven't been any better educated than mothers: wives are supposed to be happy functioning in their "natural roles." And while a woman may labor under the illusion that there's something wrong with her when she isn't constantly in a state of bliss, her husband may be inclined to feel there's something wrong with *him*—because husbands are, after all, *supposed* to make their wives happy. So, when they are presented with evidence that they don't, they may ask accusingly, "Why can't you be happy like *other* women?"

So, we are now brought to *his* side of the culturally staged battle between the sexes. First, if you work, I am hard-pressed to see that he *has* a side. However, we mustn't forget that even supportive husbands occasionally are threatened by having independent wives, and they do tend to labor under the cultural illusion that no one works harder than a man, so when his work-day ends, his home is supposed to become his castle, complete with a dutiful wife who loves being one. Actually, I don't think husbands of working wives generally are that much different in their feelings and attitudes than husbands whose wives stay home all day.

In any case, if you are a mother and a housewife, you are stuck in the house all day with the children, and your workday never ends. You struggle with the budget, and when you say you need a new dryer, he says, "We can't afford it," and then goes out and buys a boat. He doesn't understand how trying it can be to cope with and raise young children, how boring it is to keep house, or how lonely you sometimes feel when he routinely ducks behind the newspaper or becomes lost in the football game on television. (Naturally, if you work outside the home all day, you may seethe even more when he languishes in front of the TV set while you are cleaning up the dinner dishes.) He is thoughtless, inconsiderate, and seemingly indifferent. He doesn't share reponsibility for the children and he doesn't give you the support you need. He just sort of coasts through life with a "Don't-bother-me" attitude.

Yet, he is a decent person. He helps support the family and put a roof over your heads and food on the table, or perhaps even supports it totally. He doesn't beat you—indeed, he treats you, by and large, with love and respect. "What *more* do you want?" he asks. "I'm doing the best I can." Which, probably, if elaborated on, would go something like this: "I work hard every day and virtually every cent I earn goes to support this family. When I spend a little money on myself, I'm made to feel like a criminal who is taking the food out of the mouths of my children. You complain that you have no money of your own, but in reality neither have I. I don't see any end to this. I pay a doctor bill and you remind me that our children must have their teeth straightened. There's always something. I worry about what will happen to all of you if I lose my job or get sick or die. I'm glad I can give to my family, but sometimes the burden of having other people totally dependent on me is overwhelming.

"You say you never have time to do the things you want to do. Well, dammit, neither do I! I'm away from home over forty hours every week. I've had to deal with people all day and when I come home I'm tired and all I want is a little peace and quiet. But I'm expected to play the heavy with the kids from the moment I come through the door. I'm not crazy about my job, but I can't quit because I can't get as much money somewhere else. Every time I do something I enjoy, like playing golf or watching a game on TV, I feel guilty."

The stories and situations vary, of course, with some fathers loving their work and being ambitious for themselves and some hating it and being ambitious for their families. Some fathers moonlight to earn extra money to hand over to the orthodontist, and some are very involved with their children. Some are not involved on any count. But decent fathers, who are the primary wage earners, do indeed have their sides, and those sides are as valid as those of unhappy, struggling mothers.

Giving the Wage Earner Some Space

A woman once told me that the first four minutes upon waking and the first four minutes upon returning home from work were critical ones. She said that what happens during this period sets the tone for the entire day and then for the whole evening. She went on to explain that everyone needs those four minutes just to adjust to the dramatic change between sleep and wakefulness—and being out of the office and traffic and being home. Just four minutes to make a transition and collect your wits.

I believe it. Before we had children, when I was working, I came home to an empty house because generally I finished up at the office earlier than my husband did. I never fully appreciated what that meant until I became a mother and then returned briefly to a full-time job. Still the first one home, but no longer to an empty house, I would come in tired and preoccupied and instantly one sitter, two children, and one dog would descend upon me. Although I have been working at home for some time now, I can still recall having a nearly uncontrollable urge to run back, jump in the car, and drive off. All I needed was enough time to take off my coat, put my purse away, maybe go to the bathroom, look quickly through the mail, or simply do nothing. It is difficult to convey how important *not* having just a little room to make the transition from office worker to mother was to me. But I have never forgotten it. And since my husband is also my friend, and since I do my work at home and do not have to make a transition after I say hello, unless there is an emergency of some sort, I try to insure that he has space when he comes through the door in the evening. The glories and grievances we may have to share can wait until he's had a chance to take off his coat and catch his breath.

This is not to suggest that a father should be spared the reality of family life—that problems shouldn't be brought to his attention. I firmly believe that honesty is vital to any relationship. It is important for feelings to be expressed so they don't have the chance to fester, and important for *both* parents to be equally well informed about their children. Protecting a spouse from unpleasantness makes for an artificial family life and tends to exclude a father as a full-fledged member of the family. And in healthy relationships, people share their feelings, hopes, dreams, and fears. They know where they stand with each other. They know they have someone to talk it over with when things go badly—whether it's with the kids at home or with the boss at the office.

Obviously, it is more difficult either to give or receive this sort of space when *both* parents work. One suggestion for parents who take their children to sitters or to day-care centers is that they take turns picking up the kids, making it possible for each of them to enjoy a few minutes of peace and quiet every other day, before facing the evening scene. Another suggestion is to go ahead and forgo the transition period, giving each child a few minutes, and then giving each other some personal space while enjoying some quiet togetherness over a drink before starting dinner or sitting down at the table—a good idea, in any case, since I think one of the unhealthiest practices in the United States is that of going straight from the workday to the dinner table. I feel this takes some joy out of the evening and out of the dinner itself. A friend of mine, a housewife for twenty-five years, recently told me that changing her practice of having dinner on the table the minute her husband walked through the door, and instead waiting thirty minutes or so while they both sat quietly or chatted over a drink or a glass of iced tea, had improved the whole dinner scene and the evening by about 100 percent. What it is, is civilized.

Communicating

First of all, honest communication does not mean license to kill with words. As Stephani Cook noted in an article in *Glamour,* in July 1977, "Communication has become the ultimate power game . . . " Insisting that "honesty" is more abused than used, she says that "attempts to clear muddied waters too frequently result in fevered competition, in which the partners belabor . . . misdeeds and grievances in the service of 'honesty.' 'You always . . . You do . . . You are . . . Because you.'

"Simply being honest is supposed to work miracles. But getting slugged in the teeth with some juicy revelation is no more pleasant than getting slugged with a brickbat. More relationships have been picked to bits in the name of honesty than have been built . . . "[8] The point is, there is a world of difference between honesty that is necessary and honesty whose primary function, however carefully disguised, turns out to be a hurting one. Telling a spouse, for example, about an affair may relieve a guilty conscience and arouse feelings of jealousy that can be somewhat reassuring but it rarely enriches a relationship. Or, telling a husband that all your problems could be solved if he were as successful as Jane's husband or as manly as Ruth's is just another way of telling him he's inadequate. Honesty in communication means that you express your genuine feelings for the purpose of being understood and, in the process, take care to do no harm.

And while it's frequently important to get something off your chest—to clear the air—be careful about chronic complaining. When people do this they get tuned out and important complaints can be missed, or, if they are heard, not taken seriously. And it is extremely unpleasant to listen to such complaints coming from anyone. I have a friend, an otherwise nice woman, but she is negative. She complains constantly about everything. I can only take it for so long, and whatever I genuinely do enjoy about her company soon gets lost. If I had to come home to that after a day at the office, I'd think twice about coming home at all.

Nagging is even worse than chronic complaining. I put nagging other people right up there with stretching them out on the rack. It's also a waste of time and energy because usually you can't make a person do something he's not going to do by constantly nagging him about it. If on rare occasions you *do* succeed, you also get the bonus of his contempt for having tortured him. If you want a leaky faucet fixed and you ask your husband to fix it and he procrastinates, then get a book that tells you how to fix things and do it yourself, or ask someone else to do it, or call the plumber, or forget about it. Better yet, if you sense that your husband *won't* do a particular thing, don't ask him—just get it done some other way.

Another unforgivable form of communication is dredging up the past. I don't care how indignant you are or how valid your complaint might be. There is absolutely nothing that can be done to change what took place in the past. The woman who reminds her husband of the affair he had two summers ago, how he embarrassed her at a party two weeks ago by getting smashed, or how he missed making it big by not taking that good job five years ago deserves to have him retreat behind his newspaper or repair to the nearest bar. Never allowing a person to forget a past transgression is truly a sin against his person and one that should be reserved only for your very worst enemy. If you're in the habit of doing this, your husband may be gun-shy about engaging in even casual conversation with you, never knowing when something may spark your memory and get you going on a subject he would rather avoid.

But what if the situation is exactly the opposite you may be asking—it is the husband who complains, nags, dredges up the past, or accusingly uses words like "You never," and "You always." It takes two, usually, to play games. As psychiatrist Eric Berne said so long ago, if you don't want to play games, don't play them. Don't rise to the bait. When it starts, you can walk out of the room. But, you say, I'm cooking the carrots and am trapped in the kitchen. But, I say, turn off the stove and walk out of the room. If he follows you and keeps it up, you can say, "I'm not going to listen to this anymore and I think you should know that every time you start in on it I lose a little more feeling for you." It's effective if you say it calmly and *mean* it.

However, most husbands don't nag or dredge up the past. But many do something that is much worse. I have watched with absolute horror the way otherwise very decent men unconsciously demean their wives. They speak to them in a manner they would not dare use with any other human being, except possibly their children. Indeed, *I* have been involuntarily cast in the role of dingbat playing opposite the sensible, intelligent, strong man. By itself, it's annoying. It's even more annoying when you realize that treating a wife as if she's a defective is completely sanctioned by the culture. Which, of course, is one of the reasons husbands do it, frequently without thinking. The most effective way I have found for dealing with this is to say,

"Pretend I'm not your wife. Pretend I'm a co-worker or John's wife, or John himself. Now, would you care to rephrase that?"

As important as honest communication may be, there are times when silence may serve you better. For a long time, in an effort "to keep the lines of communication open," I've encouraged my husband always to say what's on his mind. Using some of the more popular techniques, when he has been as quiet as a sphinx, I'd "probe," inviting him to tell me what's bothering him. His response, "Leave me alone," would mean that he was not communicating. Gently prodding a little more elicited "LEAVE ME ALONE, DAMMIT." And then one day when I was absolutely furious about something and my son repeatedly insisted that I tell him why I was so angry, I found myself growing angrier by the minute. All I wanted was to be left in peace so that my fury could run its natural course and burn itself out— my son's questioning was interfering with that process. Thus, I finally got my husband's message. There are times when he wants to be left alone so that he can work through what's bothering him in his own way. And on those occasions what he is communicating is, "Leave me alone."

Fighting

You often hear it said that fighting is a form of communication and that it is healthy. And books and articles have been written to instruct couples in the fine art of fighting fair. While it may be true that people who have strong feelings for one another are bound to get angry and want to fight, I think that once the action gets started, the blueprints and rules fly out of the window.

And although sometimes greater understanding results from fighting, it can be very damaging to a relationship. In those instances where nothing is resolved and small angers become fanned by arguments and insults (or possibly aggravated by the fact that one of the people in the battle has read the rules and the other hasn't), one pain is simply replaced with another—or worse, added on top of an existing one. I can honestly say that after twenty years of marriage, the only emotion I ever have felt after having a fight with my husband is pain—and it can last for days and weeks. Yes, I know it's because we don't know how to fight or program our feelings. But, in truth, I'd rather concentrate on learning how *not* to become embroiled in absurd sparring matches. I'd also like someone to give me a prescription to ease the pain and depression that I cannot will myself not to feel. Probably most honest people who value their marriages will admit to a certain amount of fear that sometime there will be that last fight—the one that destroys the love of one of the partners or does irreparable damage to the relationship.

Dr. Wayne W. Dyer says, "It is time to challenge the belief" that fighting is only natural and clears the air, simply because, "You know that fighting is not a pleasant activity, and that every time it occurs, you feel miserable. In fact, fighting almost always results in a breakdown of communication, a distancing between the fighters, intensified physical reactions of increased blood pressure, stress, headaches, backaches, insomnia, and, ultimately, ulcer-producing tensions."[9]

Fights really can get out of hand. One woman, a psychologist no less, got so mad at her lover that she stomped out of the house, got into her brand-new car, which was parked behind his in the driveway, and instead of backing out and leaving—which was her original intent—shifted into first gear and rammed into his car; she put it in reverse, then in first, and did it again. And again and again.

Another woman I know, a normally easygoing, well-adjusted person, was arguing with her husband while he was driving them to a party. She became so incensed that she stepped out of a moving car.

And another. A normally nonviolent person got into it with her husband while she was chopping onions. She threatened him with a knife she was using—and later told me, "That scared me because I meant it."

A marriage counselor told me that she became so enraged at her husband while in the middle of an argument that was taking place in the living room that she jumped up and ran into the kitchen and quite literally broke every dish in the house.

According to my mother, I never threw a tantrum. At age thirty-eight, during an argument with my husband, I flung myself on the floor and kicked and pounded with my fists—on an uncarpeted hardwood floor, no less. Not only did I break a perfect record, but I nearly broke my bones in the process—I was stiff for a week.

Why do otherwise rational adults get so angry in the heat of a battle that they shed concern for the safety of themselves, their possessions, and even other people as well? Speaking for myself, the one thing that can turn me into a raving maniac is being misunderstood. The fact is, just as my husband holds opinions and possesses traits I will never fully understand, there are facets of my personality that he will never understand. And, says Dr. Dyer, the reason for this is that each of us is unique in all the world. "What that means is that no one could possibly understand you all of the time because to do so would mean they would have to become you."

Whether Dr. Dyer is correct or not, I've come to believe that when my husband and I have discussions, we should be sensitive to those times when full-scale warfare might result and back off when that danger exists. If it turns out that I am the only one so sensitive (usually true), then I must be the one to refuse to march into battle. I now diligently strive to do just that.

Respecting Each Other's Privacy

The right to privacy is guaranteed by the Constitution of the United States. Most of us cherish it for ourselves and respect it for our friends. But frequently, when it comes to the people we are married to, we actually violate federal law on more than one count. Beginning with a spouse's mail, we go against postal regulations and tamper. Next, pockets, wallets, desks, purses, and drawers are subject to search and seizure. His or her phone calls become "our" phone calls. And the person on the receiving end of this invasion of privacy is subtly denied his or her individuality.

The same applies to another person's time. As long as it is not at the expense of anyone else or in conflict with agreed-upon standards of conduct, just as a person's mail is his or her own, what he or she does with their own time is their own business. Just as a woman ought to have the right to pursue interests beyond her mothering and homemaking responsibilities and be able to arrange for the time to do so, so should her spouse. Furthermore, being able to listen to music, read, or pursue a hobby is vital to one's emotional well-being. When your husband would rather read a book, watch television, or putter in the garden instead of talking to you, don't pout and demand his undivided attention. He is a person, not a mechanical dispenser of conversation and affection.

By the way, I don't see a husband's disinterest in conversation as disinterest in his wife. I think too much has been made of this idea in recent years. Movies and soap operas are probably responsible—a favorite line seems to be, "We never talk anymore, Burt." Well, maybe when you live together and see each other every day, often there's really not that much to talk about—at least on a daily basis. I don't see the absence of a running conversation as some sort of symptom of marital discord.

Should a Wife Be a Domestic Goddess?

Well, to begin with, if she works full time outside the home, unless she swigs a case of Geritol every day and has a full-time housekeeper who also cooks the dinner and cleans up afterward, I don't see how she can be.

And now that I think about it, I don't know how it's possible for a woman who stays home all day with small children to bring it off—unless she puts the kids out for adoption and has undergone a frontal lobotomy.

While there are those who consider catering to a husband some sort of privilege and oceans of fun, as well as a sure way of "keeping your man," I find the whole idea totally revolting. The only woman I have ever known who really did this for any length of time got for her trouble a cheating husband who didn't respect her, and a case of V.D.

You are a partner in an adult relationship, not a geisha. And your husband, hopefully, is a sensible adult who would prefer respect, love, kindness, and honesty to this sort of phony con job to "get some goodies," as one advocate of such put it.

If you cater to a man there is always the danger that he might expect such treatment for the rest of your lives together, that you will get sick of it in short order and change your act, leaving him wondering about what's going on, that he will become a complete domestic cripple, or that he will lose all respect for you. Worse, of course, is the chance that you will lose all respect for yourself.

I guess I'd have to say that a woman who plays out the love-slave role is either somewhat demented or has some ulterior motive—wants something. And unless a man is utterly stupid, he can't fail to see himself as a tool, something to be manipulated for some higher purpose, but not loved for himself.

But what about being kind and considerate because you sincerely want to be? Is it subservient for a woman who stays home all day to pour her husband a cup of coffee while he's dressing for work and take it in to him? To run an errand or make a phone call that she can do with greater ease than he can? Is it subservient to pick up a copy of a book when you happen upon one he mentioned he'd like to read? Or is it thoughtful? An outward expression of affection? I think that when the basis of performing simple acts of kindness and friendship is a sincere one, these acts will be appreciated and many times returned in kind when the occasion allows. Wouldn't you do the same for a loving woman friend?

After having gone from being a traditional wife and mother for a time, and moving on to seeing every domestic issue as a political one, I've finally reached the point where I can see most things in terms of fair play, kindness, and affection.

How Do You Look?

Most people who tell you how to save your marriage or make it better, or how to improve your love life, start out by telling you how to improve your appearance so that you will be more desirable. And while my general approach might be somewhat different, I must agree that the way you look can have either a negative or positive effect on a relationship.

Working women, I think, have a distinct advantage over their peers who stay at home, when it comes to personal appearance. Although it may represent another daily annoying chore to look their best, generally speaking, working women do because they must. The woman who is out in the world gets into the habit of dressing nicely, getting her hair styled regularly, and being well groomed, seeing it as a basic requirement for the job. The fact of good grooming and general routine personal maintenance can even mask the distress she might be feeling as a result of the heavy load she's carrying.

When you are home all day it isn't difficult to slip into a routine that is less exacting than that which the average working wife automatically maintains. You don't really have to get dressed, unless, of course, you're going somewhere. And unless you're going some place special, when you do get dressed, you don't have to really do more than throw on some clothes. And if this is your habit, when your husband arrives home from work, the chances are that you aren't exactly "so nice to come home to."

I emphatically am not suggesting that you dress up to the nines for the King's arrival at the end of each day. But, how *do* you look when your husband comes home? Do you, perhaps even intentionally, look bedraggled to gain his sympathy or make him feel guilty for your hard life? Nobody wants to routinely come home to someone whose appearance says, "If it weren't for you." The way you look can be a statement—an accusation.

I think, on the other hand, if you are really striving to establish goodwill, you will attempt to look like a reasonably healthy and attractive human being who likes herself. And you will be a pleasant person to meet at the end of the day. If you're nice to come home to most of the time, on those *terrible* days when you look like you've been dragged through a knothole because you *have* been, quite likely you *will* get the sympathetic support and attention you need and deserve. The constant drudge, on the other hand, gets to be so usual that even as she listlessly threatens suicide, the response to that might well be that there is nothing to be terribly concerned about.

But more important than what your husband sees when he meets you at the end of the day is what *you* see when you look in the mirror. If the face that looks back at you is unwashed and in pain, framed with straggly hair, you're not likely to feel very good about it. Making it all look and feel better requires so little—a well-groomed body, clothes, and hair, and if you like, a touch of makeup. Topped off with an expression that gives signs that you're alive and well.

Some barriers to looking neat and well groomed, oddly, stem from ideologies that are poles apart. On the one hand, some feminists hold that doing all of the things that make a woman attractive is tantamount to surrendering to the enemy—the more militant among them insist that when women strive to look good it is because of male domination and brainwashing. On the other hand, women who have bought the whole domestic line may tend to defeminize themselves.

So often, as Nancy Friday points out in *My Mother/Myself,* once women become mothers they cease to be women. Perhaps when that happens it is owing to our fantasies of what a good mother ought to be—Madonna-like and pure. But it makes sense to consider the possibility that when we continue to be asexual long after the natal period, it is because that's the way our kids want us to be and they are able to maneuver us into it. Friday states the case well with her remembrances of her feelings toward her own mother: "The silent recriminations that she was often out for the evening, was younger than the mothers of my friends, that she didn't wear an apron and have gray hair." And then she continues her thoughts with, "We insist that mother be homey, unglamorous, like everyone else's mother."

When I look at my peers, I am able to see that quite a few children I know may well have been successful in forcing their mothers to negate their womanhood. I see women in their mid-thirties who hide their womanliness behind drab clothing, nondescript hairdos, and what I have come to see as the proper image for "mother." For what? Possibly for the dubious reward of gratitude similar to that expressed by Nancy Friday when she writes, "Then with the unfairness of children, once we have safely imprisoned her in a stereotype, we reject her as lacking excitement and jaunt off looking for someone else—someone who will be different, who will give us an idea on how to leave home, an arm to lean on while we try on our shaky new identities."[10]

Nancy Friday is talking about mothers and daughters, but it is just as true that sons are bent on de-sexing their mothers too. As one mother told me, "My son said he always resented it that I wasn't like the other mothers, and it's only now that he's nearly grown that he is able to be glad of that."

Doing the image number for your kids is getting into a no-win situation. If you are womanly, you are resented, if you're dowdy as the kids would like you to be, then you're subject to contempt. And while you may satisfy some momentary whim of your children's, it is no wonder that your husband treats you like a fixture. So why do it? You can't please your children in any case, so you may as well please yourself and please your husband too. Before you jump down my throat for that husband-pleasing suggestion, I'd like to show my true colors as a female chauvinist pig here—while I may appreciate so many nonsuperficial qualities that my own husband possesses, I've always appreciated, and even felt flattered, that *he* prides himself in his appearance. It's a two-way street. He may not look so great to please me, but then on the other hand . . .

Anyway, how do you look?

I detest joining the ranks of those who put the onus for the success or failure of a marriage on a woman. And yet, however resentfully, I must acknowledge that until we start seeing articles that tell men, "How to Save Your Marriage," or "How to Keep *Her* Interested," in *Esquire, Playboy,* or *Gentlemen's Quarterly,* and see men *reading* them, we can't expect to reverse decades of conditioning in enough time to make our own lives work better for us. Thus, if it's change we want in our marriages, it's up to us to figure out what's wrong, and what can be done about it, and then take action.

11

Perspectives

One of the most important and helpful things you can do for yourself is to begin to see how your expectations, or "shoulds," influence the quality of your life, your dissatisfactions with yourself and with others. Recognition does not occur suddenly or miraculously. You don't wake up in the middle of the night and say, "This is my problem! Now I'm going to change completely and live happily ever after for the rest of my life." Change is a gradual process. You may, of course, have a quick insight into certain situations. You may have a dream you feel is important. A friend may say something which provides food for thought. These are all opportunities to examine yourself and work with yourself.

If you have any expectations that you are going to solve your problems immediately, however, you are going to be in trouble. Be kind and gentle with yourself. Pace yourself realistically. Change is a process; health is a process. Day by day, throughout your life, you will be striving and growing.

Helen A. DeRosis
Victoria Y. Pellegrino
THE BOOK OF HOPE

Since the dawn of civilization, people have been naturally bent on problem-solving or finding better ways to do things. This is human and it is positive. But right now—and this may seem a bizarre thing to say in a book like this—I think Americans are on a solution-finding orgy that is out of control. Solution-finding is different from problem-solving, in that *problem-solving* requires that we use some initiative and resourcefulness. When we look for *solutions,* we are looking for blueprints or recipes, usually designed by some expert. A blueprint, as it stands, cannot possibly help everyone. If it is to help at all, it must encourage us to find our own ways of handling problems and our own ways of adapting certain suggestions to fit our own needs. This is what I hope this book will do—give other mothers insights and motivate them to use their own insights, combined with resourcefulness and initiative. It is not my wish to have other mothers do everything *my* way, but instead to benefit from knowing about some of the traps—those I've observed and I have fallen into—and some of the ways we have scrambled out of them.

Sometimes, when the problems are real, there are solutions. But sometimes there are no solutions beyond reconciliation and acceptance, and we all need to gain enough perspective to realize that some things can be helped and some things can't, and to know which is which. Once, long ago, the lesson in this old and unoriginal wisdom was driven home to me.

Before the development of the Salk vaccine, a relative of mine contracted polio which left him paralyzed from the neck down (only one of the many things it did to him) for the rest of his life. Although it was frequently explained—sometimes by a full battalion of professionals—that his motor nerves were as dead as doornails, many people who knew this man refused to accept that nothing could be done to restore his ability to move. It was fortunate, however, that he accepted what he was handed and thus continued his life, instead of wasting it in endless search for a nonexistent cure. He used his good mind to do good work, enjoy music, books, and the company of his family and friends. Whenever I tell this story, I can hear someone saying that he gave up hope and didn't try hard enough. Knowing full well the medical details of his case, I can only counter by saying that he gave up *false* hope, knowing that others could afford the luxury of periodically playing with the possibility that he would walk again and use his arms, but he did not want to squander the years he had left in a search that would only prove frustrating. Accepting that which could not be changed was this man's basic philosophy—and he applied it to all facets of his fully lived life.

His philosophy can easily be applied to the problems mothers have. Developing a perspective means understanding that motherhood never will be perfect and the goal of making it so is just a trap. Better to accept motherhood as a condition with ups and downs that one must learn to live with and strive to deal with rationally and realistically.

At the top of any mother's priority list must go the maintenance of her mental well-being. It is important to go back to that beginning place and remind yourself that the cultural model of motherhood virtually guarantees failure, and then periodically check that compulsion to try to emulate it, while you move on and focus on what is really important to you and your family.

If you want or need a creative outlet, consider that a valid need, for indeed it is. Without my creative outlets, I become cranky and depressed, and I think that's true of many people. One woman told me that she regularly tells her children, "You get between me and my art, and you're really in trouble." She considers being kept from her painting an assault on her very being. For those who might say, "Yes, but having children is creative," I say, yes, by definition, it is the ultimate in creation—but caring for children isn't necessarily a creative outlet for everyone.

If you need to work outside the home to maintain your sanity, because you need the money, or just because you want to, *do* it. Although the idea of women fulfilling themselves in ways that have nothing to do with their traditional motherhood roles is becoming more socially acceptable, it is difficult to overcome years of conditioned reflexes and a predisposition toward guilt over working at an outside job, no matter how much reinforcement has existed in recent years. Naturally, the backlash created by Phyllis Schlafly and her gang has made it tougher for some mothers. But when you listen to their rhetoric, remind yourself that while they preach that a woman's place is in the home, they usually are not home when they are out doing their preaching.

If you have any hesitation over the woman's-place-is-in-the-home argument, and have a daughter, try thinking of her in those terms. Frankly, I want my daughter to have more options than that, and if I were willing to take less for myself, I could not begin to convey to her that she might have those options—which is not to say that were she to select full-time homemaking I think she would be wrong. That is her option. But let it be an option, not her only way to exist.

Whether or not a mother chooses to work outside the home or be a homemaker, striving to be a perfect mother is folly. Sacrificing by filling the days with unnecessary domestic and child-related activities, all of which come before any actual needs of the mother, ignores what really is essential to a child's needs and gets the priorities all out of whack. Right up at the top of the list and of equal weight to your mental well-being is the well-being of your children. They need sane parents, love, nutrition, shelter, medical care, the teaching of values and integrity—and if *yours* are good, the task generally requires little more than serving as a model. Everything else is a frill. Teaching a three-year-old to read when he or she will learn to do so in preschool or elementary school is necessary only if your educational system is deficient. The same applies to enriching experiences, the fun of which can easily evaporate for everyone when recreation is seen as a duty. Making sacrifices that need not be made so that you later can cut down your child with, "After all I've done for you . . ." doesn't make sense.

Some people feel that children are truly deprived if they don't have pets; then they wind up having to take care of animals when they may already have too many beings to care for (yes, I know all about pets being the responsibility of the children, but it still is mother who is home with them when the kids are out or in school, and mother who has to drive the animal to the vet). A child is *not* deprived if you decide that a dog or cat or even a goldfish is too much trouble for you. Pets to children are like toys—kids love their stuffed teddy bears nearly as much as they love real live animals.

I will never forget, for example, Lisa's devotion to "Snoopy." Nothing would do until she had a Snoopy that you could buy clothes for. She would dress and undress the dog, talk to it, brush it—even wash it with upholstery cleaner. At one point she became adamant that Snoopy needed some new clothes. I thought perhaps she was becoming a little eccentric until once, when we were going on vacation (with Snoopy along, of course), I saw a family come into the airport and noticed that the mother was carrying a Snoopy just like ours. She sat down for a moment, absently adjusted Snoopy's aviator cap and smoothed out some wrinkles in his flying jacket. When it was time to leave, she got up, holding Snoopy like a baby, and her son (who was about ten years old) admonished her, "Don't hold him too tight. He doesn't like it." Mother dutifully relaxed her grip. The boy then nodded his approval. There is a funny moral here: not only do children think of stuffed animals as live beings, but whether the pets are alive or stuffed, mother somehow always winds up taking care of them.

Although I promised that there is light at the end of the tunnel, when the youngest child starts school, the light does not shine as brightly as it could for some mothers who trade off the pressures of constant mothering for pressures of a different order.

At the present time over half of all American mothers work. However, if I used Palo Alto as my frame of reference, I would find that statistic unbelievable. The mother with children in school who might have interests beyond full-time motherhood is totally invisible in this community. The unwritten code is that all mothers *participate*. They work as volunteers in the school library or on school carnivals; they work as teachers' aides in the classroom, they go on field trips, they are active in the PTA. They are similarly active in Brownies, Bluebirds, Campfire Girls, Scouts and Little League.

Those who are truly dedicated spend their "off duty" hours observing in the classroom so that they can see that their children are learning. I know mothers who do this on a daily basis (and teachers who wish they wouldn't). Then, of course, there are swimming lessons, dancing lessons, soccer lessons, and music lessons to be seen to once school lets out. For the active mother, there is no light at the end of the tunnel—she may not be trapped in the house with preschoolers all day, but if she's truly dedicated she doesn't spend much time in her house at all because she spends most of it either at the school or on the road!

One summer day, for example, when I took Lisa to the orthodontist's office, I ran into a mother I know who greeted me with, "How are you surviving the summer?" After telling her I thought I was holding my own, I turned the question to her. "Well," she said, "I'm really busy—we're up early every morning for Billy's tennis and then I take Mark to swim meet. Then there are the flute lessons and gymnastics in the afternoon, and with everything so tightly scheduled, I have to drive all over because if they took the bus they'd be late. Besides, I really should be there to watch. And, oh, yes, there's soccer and camping about every weekend. What it really means is that I give up my whole summer."

Like one of Pavlov's dogs I responded as I was supposed to. The familiar guilty twinge was there.

As I sat listening to Billy's and Mark's mother talk, the twinge started turning into a knot. And then a little light went on when she said, "I don't know what I'd do if there were more children in this family." My thoughts turned immediately to my friend Alice, the mother of eight children. Alice, understandably, is not that heavily involved with her children and their activities. How could she be? Alice's children are about as happy, healthy, and bright as kids can be. They are very resourceful when it comes to knowing what to do with themselves. Thoughts moved on to other mothers who don't exist to serve their children—mothers who work outside the home, for instance, who couldn't possibly give up whole summers, or even chunks of them, to devote themselves exclusively to the enrichment of their children. Yet neither their children nor my own are deprived, neglected, or unloved. The knot that had been a twinge in my stomach left.

The futility of sacrificing oneself for the superficial, socially acceptable pursuits of mothering, and leaving nothing for oneself, was reinforced often after that day.

I well remember Bryan's mother—Supermom. She was taking her children on some rather involved outing and had invited Adam to go along with them. When she came by to pick up my son, we chatted for a few minutes and in that brief space of time I learned that this mother worked as a volunteer three mornings a week at her younger child's nursery school and five afternoons a week at the elementary school; that immediately after school every day she drove the children to their music or gymnastic classes; that during every spring and winter break she and her husband took the children camping or skiing; that the entire summer was so completely planned that, regrettably, her boys probably wouldn't be able to spend much time with Adam. Also, this mother worked on the school newsletter, was active in the PTA, a room mother, and was planning to be a den mother in the fall. And she always asked for extra time during parent-teacher conferences so she could really cover every aspect of her children's progress and constructively "interface" with the teacher. Making matters worse—for me at least—she apparently loved spending so much time doing all these child-related things.

About a week after our first meeting, Supermom came by to drop off Bryan to play with Adam. After she left, I was appropriately depressed about my maternal deficiencies and dragged around the house, trying to work up some enthusiasm for cleaning it. At some point I became aware that Bryan was following me around quite a lot. Then Adam started following me too, complaining that Bryan wouldn't play with him. The two of them got into an argument, and the boy called his mother and she came to pick him up.

Bryan came over once more before the summer marathon was

to begin. He had been here for an hour when he called for his mother to come and get him. After they left, I asked Adam if he and Bryan had gotten into a fight. He insisted that they really hadn't, but that Bryan didn't want to play. It was then that I realized that Bryan didn't know *how* to play—I recalled the day a week before when he'd followed me around. This child's life was so organized that he didn't know what to do with unstructured time.

Today Bryan and his younger brother are both in a special school. It seems that both boys have difficulty in class because they need a one-to-one arrangement in order to learn. They are extremely nervous children and can't tolerate the normal classroom situation.

What our culture has done to a simple biological role has been to make it incredibly complicated, leaving very little space for parents to experience some of the true joys that can be found in our children. Society tells us many of those joys are such things as being proud when a child performs well or turns out well. Well, what if he or she *doesn't? What then?*

The accomplishments of our children really have nothing to do with us. *They* own their own accomplishments. *We* do not— their successes are not reflections of what glorious parents we are. Nor are any of their failures a sure indication that they have pulled duds for parents.

No child in this family ever will get bawled out for pulling a bad grade in school or having an off day in sports. I believe that when a parent reprimands a child for not doing well either in the classroom or on the baseball field it's because the parent is under pressure to demonstrate worth through the child's accomplishments. Without such pressure I think parents probably would fall back on their instincts and common sense and know when a child needs support and compassion instead of criticism.

Common sense would likely tell them that their child was underprepared, over his or her head, or under too much pressure from himself or herself.

When we parents see our children not as *our* children but as individual *people*, we then are able to see ourselves as people too, rather than mere instruments.

Part of the joy I have learned to find in my children comes from my recognition that Lisa and Adam aren't really "mine." They are separate human beings. Their purpose in life is not to reflect well on their parents (also separate human beings), but, instead, to live their own lives. The role of the mother and father is to nurture and nourish them and guide them the best way we know how—accepting responsibility for the things that really count while we keep *our* egos out of the entire matter.

Proving that I can fulfill the cultural role of motherhood proves nothing. It surely doesn't prove love. There certainly is a need to demonstrate it, but *proving* it has no place in a genuinely loving relationship.

The children who have been entrusted to our care give us a unique opportunity to love unconditionally and purely. Only when we are able to cut through all of the superficial claptrap about motherhood are we truly able to experience loving our young. It goes all the way back to that moment of awe and wonder when they came into our lives, separate and unique.

Not long ago, when I gave a talk to a group of mothers, I was asked what I hoped for during the next years—specifically what I hoped for during my children's adolescent years. First, I said that I hoped our marriage would endure and that our home would give each member of our family the stability and security we need, and that my husband and I would have the wisdom and compassion necessary for getting through these years of dramatic change. Next, I said, I fervently hoped that the children I love more than any others on earth would make it through those bizarre and emotional years with a minimum of pain, emotional stress, and physical damage. There are trying times ahead for them, and for us too because we hurt when they hurt. It will be wonderful, when the returns are in, if our children make it to adulthood relatively unscarred. I want them to arrive at their adulthood physically and emotionally healthy, with the same zest for life they now have.

When I look at the goals I have for the children, I am able to feel that it is perfectly okay to be simply a nurturing mother— to provide my son and daughter with love, understanding, guidance, food, shelter, and medical care. I can feel that it is perfectly fine for mothers who find satisfaction in doing so to go beyond that—to be quite involved in their children's lives. Such a perspective allows me to feel that it is no longer necessary to equate our different interests as inadequacy or neurosis in order to justify their activities or my lack of similar ones. The only time I can truly object to Supermother is when she tries to pressure other mothers into accepting her standards and feeling guilty if they don't or can't.

At this moment I'm the best mother I know how to be. It may not be someone else's ideal; I never will be perfect and I will continue to make mistakes before I'm retired from this job. But I am *there* as fully realized as I can be to shepherd my children. My love for them is as deep as love ever can be. My commitment to them—to our family—is as complete as my commitment to myself, and vice versa. Everyone here can count on me for the important things I can give—and they know it. More important is that *I* know it. And I know it works both ways.

We are, Cal and I, neither slaves nor slave owners. We are *stewards*. And that, I think, is what motherhood—and parenthood—finally is all about.

Notes

Chapter Two

1 From an interview with Patty Ginsburg, March 2, 1977, in the Palo Alto *Times,* pp. 33–34.
2 Harry Brown, *How I Found Freedom in an Unfree World,* Macmillan Publishing Co., New York, 1973, p. 39.

Chapter Three

1 The Boston Women's Health Book Collective, *Our Bodies, Ourselves,* Simon and Schuster, New York, 1976, pp. 44, 47.
2 Margaret Mead, *Blackberry Winter, My Earlier Years,* William Morrow, New York, 1972, p. 49.
3 Jessie Bernard, *The Future of Motherhood,* Dial Press, New York, 1974, p. 49.
4 *Human Behavior Magazine,* February 1978, p. 61.

Chapter Four

1 *San Francisco Chronicle,* December 8, 1977; from an article by Dr. Robert B. Howard, writing in *Postgraduate Medicine,* p. 78.
2 Kenneth Keniston and the Carnegie Council on Children, *All Our Children: The American Family Under Pressure,* Harcourt Brace Jovanovich, New York, 1977, pp. 86–87.
3 Arlene Skolnick, "The Myth of the Vulnerable Child," *Psychology Today,* February 1978, p. 97
4 Benjamin Spock, *Baby and Child Care,* Pocket Books, New York, 1968, pp. 101–102.
5 Arlene Skolnick, *op. cit.,* pp. 114–115.

Chapter Five

1 Fitzhugh Dodson, *How to Parent,* Nash Publishing Company, Los Angeles, California, 1970, pp. 121–122.
2 Benjamin Spock, *Baby and Child Care,* Pocket Books, New York, 1968, p. 122.
3 Theodore Isaac Rubin, *The Angry Book,* Macmillian Publishing Co., New York, 1969, p. 126.
4 Angela Barron McBride, *A Married Feminist,* Harper and Row, New York, 1975, p. 128.
5 Paul Wood and Bernard Schwartz, "I Mean *Now,*" *Psychology Today,* July 1977, p. 131.
6 Angela Barron McBride, *op. cit.,* p. 137.

Chapter Seven

1 James R. Dobson, *Hide or Seek,* Fleming R. Revell Company, Old Tappan, New Jersey, 1974, p. 187.

Chapter Eight

1 "The Changing American Family," *The New York Times,* reprinted in the *San Francisco Chronicle,* December 29, 1977, p. 196.
2 Jane Whitbread, "How Will Your Kids Turn Out When You're Away All Day?" *Working Woman,* November 1977, p. 200.
3 Among the articles that review various studies that show that when mothers work their children do not suffer are: Margie Norman, "Substitutes for Mother," *Human Behavior,* February 1978; Constance Rosenblum, "Should Mother Work Outside the Home?" New York *News,* April 19, 1978, p. 200.
4 United Press International, March 12, 1975, p. 205.
5 *Redbook,* May 1978, p. 214.

Chapter Ten

1 Richard B. Austin, Jr., *How to Make It with Another Person: Getting Close, Staying Close*, Macmillan Publishing Co., New York, 1976, pp. 267–268.

2 David Viscott, *How to Live with Another Person*, Arbor House, New York, 1975, pp. 271–272.

3 E. E. LeMasters, "Parenthood as Crisis," *Marriage and Family Living*, Vol. 19, No. 4, 1957, p. 275.

4 Arthur P. Jacoby, "Transition to Parenthood: A Reassessment," *Journal of Marriage and the Family*, Vol. 26, 1964.

5 Harold Feldman, "Changes and Parenthood: A Methodological Design," unpublished study, Cornell University, p. 276.

6 Richard B. Austin, Jr., *op. cit.*, p. 276.

7 Jessie Bernard, *The Future of Marriage*, World Publishing Company, New York, 1972, p. 277.

8 Stephani Cook, "The Right Way to Ask," *Glamour*, July 1977, pp. 285–287.

9 Wayne W. Dyer, "Family Fights," *San Francisco Chronicle*, October 10, 1977, p. 292.

10 Nancy Friday, *My Mother/Myself: The Daughter's Search for Identity*, Delacorte, New York, 1977, p. 302.